D1103795

QUESNAY'S TABLEAU ÉCONOMIQUE
A CRITIQUE AND REASSESSMENT

QUESNAY'S TABLEAU ÉCONOMIQUE

A CRITIQUE AND REASSESSMENT

STEVEN PRESSMAN
Monmouth College

AUGUSTUS M. KELLEY PUBLISHERS

Published by Augustus M. Kelley, Publishers
Fairfield NJ 07004

Library of Congress Cataloging-in-Publication Data

Pressman, Steven.
   Quesnay's Tableau économique : a critique and
reassessment / Steven Pressman. — 1st ed.
   Includes bibliographical references and index.
   ISBN 0-678-01471-X
   1. Quesnay, François, 1694-1774. Tableau économique.
2. Economics—Mathematical models—History. I. Title.
HB 153.Q582P74   1994   94-21389
330.15´2—dc20

For Jane, with whom I have always gone back and forth.

PREFACE

This book grew out of a term paper that I wrote for Robert Heilbroner's Development of Economic Thought course in the Fall of 1979. That paper attempted to explain Quesnay's static or stationary model. My treatment of the *Tableau* subsequently expanded to include concern with dynamic versions of the *Tableau* and with policy applications of the *Tableau*, and quickly became my doctoral dissertation. This book constitutes an expansion and revision of that work.

While writing my original paper on the *Tableau* and expanding it into this book I have incurred a large number of debts. First, I am indebted to my colleague Howard Nitzberg, currently Professor of English and Foreign Languages at Monmouth College. Howard spent many evenings with me pouring over passages in French written by Quesnay, and trying to help me make sense of them. Without Howard's patience and dedication, my knowledge of Quesnay and the *Tableau* would have been lacking, and this work would have been worse for it.

Robert Heilbroner, Ray Majewski, Edward Nell, Ross Thomson, and Thomas Vietorisz all read early versions of this work. Their questions, critical comments, and remarks have significantly improved the quality of this book.

Finally, I am also indebted to the Princeton and Yale University libraries for granting me access to their rare book collections, to Monmouth College for granting me liberal release time from teaching in order to finish this book, and to Jeanne Martino and Diana Prout for typing the final manuscript.

vii

TABLE OF CONTENTS

LIST OF FIGURES

Figure   Page

xi

Figure		Page

CHAPTER I
INTRODUCTION

Over the years, opinion has been sharply divided regarding Quesnay's *Tableau Économique*. Some economists have felt the development of the *Tableau* to be a major theoretical achievement, shedding immense light on the economic process. Others have ignored or ridiculed it. Numerous instances of these diverse opinions can be provided.

Quesnay's Physiocratic colleague and collaborator, the Marquis de Mirabeau, listed the *Tableau*, along with the inventions of writing and money, as one of the three greatest discoveries ever made. Moreover, the *Tableau* was singled out by Mirabeau for special praise because it completed and perfected the other two discoveries.[1]

Adam Smith was also impressed with the *Tableau*. As is well-known, Smith did criticize the *Tableau* for employing a number of unrealistic assumptions. His main complaint was that the class of artificers, manufacturers and merchants was assumed to be barren and unproductive, although the wealth of the nation was greater due to these workers. Because they contributed to a nation's wealth, Smith concluded that these workers were not sterile. Smith also objected to considering artificers, manufacturers and merchants in the same category as menial servants. The former replenish their wage fund; the latter cause the wage fund of their masters to be depleted. However, despite these objections, Smith declared that the Tableau "with all its imperfections is, perhaps, the nearest approximation to the truth that has yet been published upon the subject of political economy.[2]"

While the Tableau was highly regarded in the early 1770's, following the demise of Physiocracy in 1776—the year that Turgot lost the office of comptroller of general finances for France—it was

---

[1] Francois Quesnay, *Philosophie Rurale* (Amsterdam: Chez Les Libraires Associés, 1764), Volume 1, pp. 52-53. This remark has been made famous by Adam Smith, and is quoted in Adam Smith, *The Wealth of Nations* (New York: Modern Library, 1937), p. 643.

[2] Smith, *Wealth of Nations*, p. 642.

1

virtually ignored for 100 years. The great works of political economy following *The Wealth of Nations* all fail to take note of Quesnay and the *Tableau*. There is no mention of the *Tableau* in Ricardo's Principles of Political Economy and Taxation, in Malthus' *Principles of Political Economy*, in James Mill's *Elements of Political Economy*, or in John Stuart Mill's *Principles of Political Economy*.

It was not until Marx resurrected Quesnay that economists again seriously considered the *Tableau*. Marx himself regarded it as the forerunner to his simple reproduction model. Two chapters of *Theories of Surplus Value* are devoted to an explanation and analysis of the *Tableau* and the doctrines of Physiocracy. These pages are filled with great praise for the *Tableau*, culminating in Marx's opinion that the Tableau "was an extremely brilliant conception".[3]

However, Marx's contemporary, Eugen Dühring, was of an entirely different opinion. Dühring criticized and mocked the *Tableau*, believing it nothing but an amalgam of confused and arbitrary conceptions bordering on mysticism. In addition, he thought the *Tableau*'s figures were the result of a mathematical fantasy on the part of Quesnay. The entire enterprise Dühring compared with attempts to square the circle.[4]

This dichotomy of opinion has continued into the twentieth century. Alfred Marshall accused the Physiocrats of confusing causal laws and ethical principles of conformity to Nature. This, Marshall believed, made the *Tableau* of little direct value.[5] More recently, the *Tableau* has been dismissed for being both obscure and inconsistent. Sir Alexander Gray views the *Tableau* as an embarrassing footnote to Physiocracy. "Despite Dupont's assurance that the *Tableau Économique* is obscure only to those who are lacking in the power of comprehension, it may be doubted whether it will ever be anything but a vast mystification, a subject to be treated gingerly by commentators, rendered uneasy by the feeling that they do not quite understand what they are talking about".[6] Gray's sentiment here is

---

[3] Karl Marx, *Theories of Surplus Value* (Moscow: Foreign Language Publishing House, no date), p. 334.

[4] These remarks are reported in Fredrich Engels, *Herr Eugen Dühring's Revolution in Science* (New York: International Publishers, no date), p. 276.

[5] Alfred Marshall, *Principles of Economics*, 8th ed. (New York: Macmillan and Co., 1947), p. 756.

[6] Sir Alexander Gray and Alan Thompson, *The Development of Economic Doctrine*, 2nd ed. (New York: Longman, 1980), p. 93.

echoed by Guy Routh, who writes: "Like Keynes' *General Theory*
Quesnay's ... writings owed their prestige in part to their obscurity",[7]
and by Harry Landreth, who in his textbook the *History of Economic
Theory*, accuses Physiocracy of being deficient in both logic and
detail.[8]   Finally, Paul Samuelson has recently equated the *Tableau*
with "mystification and abracadabra".[9]

Against these negative comments we can juxtapose a number
of favorable recent views.   Wassily Leontief has claimed that the
Tableau was an important precursor of his input-output analysis,[10]
a sentiment that has been echoed by a large number of commentators.[11]

Gram and Walsh call the *Tableau* "a great turning point in
the development of classical analysis," which profoundly influenced
the reproduction schemes of Marx, and "in the twentieth century, the
development of general equilibrium models of the classical type, such
as those of [von] Neumann and Sraffa."[12]   E.K. Hunt praises the
Tableau for anticipating Malthus, Marx, and Keynes in showing how
problems in the circulation process could create economic crises, and
for laying the foundation for the distinction between productive and
unproductive labor, which became the cornerstone of 19th century
economic analysis.[13]   Schumpeter also praised the *Tableau* for its
analytic novelties.   He singled out as especially noteworthy its
separation of production and distribution into separate processes, the
fact that the *Tableau* opened up the possibility of numerical analysis,
and the fact that the *Tableau* was the first attempt to convey the
notion of equilibrium.[14]   Finally, Ronald Meek extols the *Tableau*

---

[7] Guy Routh, *The Origin of Economic Ideas* (New York: Random House, 1975, p. 71.

[8] Harry Landreth, *History of Economic Theory* (Boston: Houghton Mifflin, 1976), p. 26.

[9] Paul A. Samuelson, "Quesnay's 'Tableau Economique' as a Theorist would formulate it Today," in *Classical and Marxian Political Economy*, ed. Ian Bradley and Michael Howard (New York: St. Martin's Press, 1982), p. 47.

[10] Wassily Leontief, *The Structure of the American Economy, 1919-1929* (Cambridge: Harvard University Press, 1941), p. 2.

[11] See the references in Chapter V.

[12] Harvey Gram and Vivian Walsh, *Classical and Neoclassical Theories of General Equilibrium* (New York: Oxford University Press, 1980), p. 28.

[13] E.K. Hunt, *History of Economic Thought: A Critical Perspective* (Belmont: Wadsworth, 1979), p. 32f.

[14] Joseph A. Schumpeter, *History of Economic Analysis* (New York: Oxford University Press, 1954), p. 241f.

as the precursor of a number of modern methods of economic analysis. In addition to foreshadowing general equilibrium and input-output analyses, Meek contends that Quesnay's zig-zags are similar to the Keynesian multiplier and that the Physiocratic analysis of hoarding is similar to the famous paradox of thrift. He concludes:

> The *Tableau* is far from being the ideal and airy thing which it is sometimes made out to be: on the contrary, it is one of the most striking examples in the whole history of economic thought of the achievement of a harmonious unity between abstract theory and concrete investigation. And if we add that it also embodied a fairly advanced understanding of the key causal significance of relations between socio-economic groups, it should become clear that it is not only economic antiquarians who can benefit from its study.[15]

A distinct pattern reveals itself here. Condemnation of the *Tableau* has focused on its obscurity, especially its mathematical obfuscation; praise has stressed the *Tableau*'s foreshadowing of modern ideas and forms of analysis. While these opinions may seem contradictory, this is not necessarily so. Praise has been heaped on Quesnay's vision; criticism has been placed on the particulars of his model. The mathematics of the *Tableau* have thus hindered a full appreciation of its achievements.

This is in sharp contrast to the usual role of mathematics in economic theory. Most of the time mathematical and numerical examples *add* persuasiveness to an economic theory. For example, the arithmetic and geometric progressions of Malthus' *Essay on Population* gave dramatic precision to Malthus' vision of impending overpopulation.

Just as mathematical models can support an economist's vision, they can also detract from that vision. This is most likely to occur when the mathematics of the model is itself the subject of confusion and debate. Concern about obscure or fictitious mathematics then carries over into skepticism regarding the initial vision, and leads to hasty dismissal of a model for being confused. It is this problem which has plagued Quesnay's *Tableau*, and provides a plausible explanation for the diversity of opinion regarding the

---

[15] Ronald Meek, *The Economics of Physiocracy* (Cambridge: Harvard University, 1963), p. 295f.

Tableau and Physiocracy.

A number of factors contribute to the confusion surrounding the mathematics of the *Tableau*. In the first place, Quesnay frequently falls into mathematical errors. Second, the *Tableau* lacks a certain mathematical sophistication, thus putting later economists ill at ease. The numerical values are presented with no explanation detailing how they were derived, and Quesnay provides no algebraic formulas which might allow the reader to reproduce his figures. Recent attempts at making the *Tableau* more sophisticated mathematically—putting the zig-zags into algebraic notation and converting the *Tableau* into a Leontief input-output model—have accordingly improved the esteem of the *Tableau*. A third source of confusion stems from the fact that the *Tableau* is just a small part of Quesnay's model. Intrasectoral transactions are ignored; the state and foreign trade are excluded; no provision is made for capital depreciation; and transactions involving raw materials are excluded from zig-zag versions of the *Tableau*. Fourth, Quesnay did not help his case by setting forth a number of different versions of the *Tableau*. These break down in a number of ways. Some presentations employ the famous zig-zags. Other versions—the précis and formula—shun the zig-zags, and summarize all the relations represented by the zig-zags with one intersectoral transaction. Continuity between these different versions of the *Tableau* is assumed, but never demonstrated. Quesnay also employed the *Tableau* to show both simple reproduction and reproduction with economic growth and decline. The former are the static versions of the *Tableau*; the latter are the dynamic versions. The relationship between them is left unexplained by Quesnay. Finally, at crucial junctures Quesnay fails to be clear about the assumptions and mechanisms that he is employing. All attempts at understanding the *Tableau* must at some point run up against these ambiguities.

This work will attempt to bridge the gap between the diametrically opposed evaluations of the *Tableau*. On the one hand, I will attempt to show that the *Tableau* does not involve any sort of mystification—that it is a coherent mathematical model rather than a mathematical fantasy. On the other hand, I will argue that Quesnay's contribution was not merely the foreshadowing of contemporary modes of economic analysis. The *Tableau* is a remarkable achievement in its own right. In an era when economists are breast fed on models it is hard to appreciate the immense intellectual leap that resulted in the *Tableau*. Not only did Quesnay conceptualize the notion of an economic model, an outstanding idea by itself, but he then went ahead and actually developed a model. Surprisingly, the model was not a simple and rudimentary one. Quite the contrary, the *Tableau* possesses a richness which few, if any, of its successors have captured.

The following chapters will attempt to demystify the *Tableau* and pave the way for a thorough appreciation of its profound achievement. This will be accomplished for the most part by clearly setting forth assumptions and mechanisms of the *Tableau*, and demonstrating how the *Tableau* operates. Chapter III examines the static versions of the *Tableau*. This chapter will look at *Tableaux* showing reproduction without growth or decline, and will explain the principles of this model. Chapter IV does the same things with respect to the dynamic versions of the *Tableau*. In Chapter V we will look at various attempts to explain the *Tableau* as an input-output model, as well as the claims of those economists who praise the *Tableau* because it presages input-output models. Chapter VI deals with applications of the *Tableau*. We will look at a number of uses to which Quesnay put the *Tableau*, and attempt to explain his analysis and examples. Here the practical, policy-related side of the *Tableau* will come to the fore. Finally, Chapter VII will bring together the issues noted earlier in this chapter. We will look at the *Tableau* in relation to succeeding reproduction schemes and models. We will also return to the issue of evaluating Quesnay and the *Tableau*. But first, we must look at the development of the *Tableau* itself—its different presentations and the changes which Quesnay incorporated into succeeding versions. This will be the subject of the next chapter.

CHAPTER II
THE DEVELOPMENT OF THE *TABLEAU*

The idea that production and distribution takes place in an orderly fashion forms the basis of the *Tableau Économique*. Such a notion did not originate with Quesnay however. Richard Cantillon's *Essay*, with which Quesnay was familiar, already contained the idea of circular flow relations between the different sectors or classes of society.

Quesnay's contribution was not the formulation of this idea, but its formalization. By setting forth production and distribution relations in a table, Quesnay made a significant advance beyond the verbal descriptions of Cantillon. The idea of a circular flow was thereby made precise and given substance. Numerical values incorporated into the table gave the *Tableau* persuasiveness. Formalization also enabled Quesnay to see a number of additional uses for his model. Sometime between publication of the second and third editions, Quesnay saw that the *Tableau* could be used to illustrate reproduction in growing and declining economies, as well as reproduction relations in a static economy. Naturally, the causes of economic growth and decline become important once their effects could be shown using the *Tableau*. Also, economic policies could be analyzed in terms of their effects on circulation and production. The development and possible applications of the dynamic *Tableau* at once became Quesnay's major concern.

In this chapter we will examine the development of the *Tableau* itself. We begin, in Section I, with the early *Encyclopedia* articles. We will see where and how these articles contain principles that were later incorporated into the *Tableau*. Section II deals with the three editions of the *Tableau*. These are all static models employing Quesnay's famous zig-zags. Finally, Section III looks at Quesnay's dynamic *Tableaux*. These are presented in a number of different places, and are used for several different purposes. Quesnay's later works—*L'Ami des Hommes, Philosophie Rurale*, and the "First and Second Economic Problem"—all contain dynamic *Tableaux*. These *Tableaux* are designed to analyze a number of different phenomena—price changes, tax policy, the effect of consuming too many manufactured goods or too many agricultural

7

goods, etc. In what follows we will set forth Quesnay's assumptions and his presentation of the *Tableau.* Our concern will be with examining what Quesnay said and what changes he made in the *Tableau* over time. In addition, some of the ambiguities and problems of the model will be touched on. Subsequent chapters will attempt to deal with these difficulties, and to clearly explain the model and Quesnay's analysis of the causes of economic growth and decline.

SECTION I

Quesnay's first economic publications were three articles, written between 1756 and 1757, that Diderot published in his *Encyclopedia.*

One of these, "Corn," was intended as a polemic against mercantilism and in favor of free trade. Free trade in corn, especially the export of corn for manufactured goods, was not consistent with mercantilist doctrines. The import of manufactured goods meant that specie would leave the domestic economy to pay for these manufactures. Because the mercantilists took specie to be wealth, the import of manufactured goods had to impoverish a nation. The export of corn was also opposed by mercantilists. This, they thought, would lead to domestic shortages. Free trade in corn thus ran counter to the mercantilist "policy of provision."[16]

Quesnay's arguments in "Corn" were designed to show the benefits of free trade. His main argument was that free trade in corn would increase both exports of corn and the domestic production of corn. The French economy would produce relatively more corn and relatively less manufactured goods according to Quesnay. The men and inputs used previously to produce manufactured goods will find employment in agriculture. Production in the manufacturing sector though is sterile; "the artisan destroys in the form of subsistence as much as he produces by his labor."[17] No increase in wealth can occur when manufactured goods are produced. In contrast, "agricultural work compensates for the costs involved, pays for the manual labor employed in cultivation, provides gains for the husbandman and, in addition, produces the revenue of landed

---

[16] See Eli F. Heckscher, *Mercantilism* (London: George Allen & Unwin Ltd, 1933) Vol. II, pp. 80-112.

[17] Ronald L. Meek, *Economics of Physiocracy*, p. 73.

property."[18]   Here we find the first statement of the Physiocratic doctrine that only the agricultural sector will produce a surplus. Moreover, Quesnay notes that this fact is not a consequence of the different wages paid in different economic sectors. Wages in both the agricultural and manufacturing sectors are limited to the subsistence needs of workers. In the *Tableau*, this becomes Quesnay's assumption that per capita consumption is that same in both the manufacturing and the agricultural sectors.

Greater surpluses, due to development of the agricultural sector, have additional benefits. They raise the revenue of the proprietor. And it is the demand of the proprietors that, when circulated, causes production to increase and wealth, or a net product, to be generated. Quesnay writes: "the revenue ought to be spent in order that it may be circulated annually among the whole people and provide funds for the state."[19]   This passage contains, albeit in rudimentary form, the fundamental idea of the *Tableau*. It is the demand of the proprietors, and in turn demand by the two producing classes, that determines the output and wealth of a nation.

Of course, Quesnay's vision is not fully developed at this stage. He unfortunately fails to explain the mechanism whereby an increase in demand results in increased production. Likewise, there is no discussion of the actual circulation process, and no clear understanding of the relationship between circulation and production which provides the foundation of the *Tableau*. These all come later.

Quesnay's second *Encyclopedia* article, "Men" was concerned with population. The article is an investigation into the size and distribution of the population, and an inquiry into the factors causing population to decline. In the course of studying population, Quesnay moves a step closer to developing an economic table. A circulation mechanism, foreshadowing the exchange relations of the *Tableau*, is described. The three classes or sectors that comprise the *Tableau* are clearly defined and distinguished. But it is population that is foremost in Quesnay's mind.

Population is important because "it is men who constitute the power of states." Moreover, "it is upon the employment of men and the increase of population that the maintenance and expansion of the successively regenerated wealth of nations depend."[20]   This makes

---

[18] Ibid., p. 72.
[19] Ibid., p. 76.
[20] Ibid., p. 88.

it incumbent to understand the factors tending to increase and decrease the population of a state.

The prime factor affecting population is the revenue of a nation. "The population of a state increases in the proportion that the nation's revenue increases, because the revenue procures well-being and gains by which men are maintained and attracted."[21] Revenue alone, however, is not sufficient to increase population. It is also necessary that the revenue be spent. Only spent revenues— what economists today call effective demand—employ men. Only spent revenues provide income to maintain men and attract workers from foreign nations. This principle becomes, as we shall see, a key mechanism of Quesnay's dynamic *Tableaux.*

Besides studying the factors that contribute to or detract from a nation's population, "Men" also contains a description of the population. Quesnay divides the population of a nation into three distinct sectors or classes—a sterile class, which produces manufactured goods; a class of proprietors or landlords; and a productive class, which produces agricultural goods. This three-fold distinction becomes part of all editions of the *Tableau.*

The manufacturing class consists, in part, of manufacturers of cloth, cobblers, servants, cooks, and musicians. They are paid out of a wage fund, and the value of their produce equals the cost of their labor and raw materials. Because no surplus or wealth is created by this class, Quesnay dubbed the manufacturing class "sterile." Also included in the manufacturing class are individuals who trade goods abroad—importers and exporters. Contrary to the mercantilists, Quesnay believed that foreign trade could never result in gains or surpluses for a nation. All traders must therefore also be part of the sterile class.

A second class consists of all groups that receive revenues but do not engage in productive activity. Quesnay distinguishes three such groups. Landlords receive revenues in the form of rent; the sovereign receives revenues in the form of taxes; and the clergy receives revenues in the form of tithes. The landlords, the sovereign, and the clergy are lumped together by Quesnay based upon their similar roles in the reproduction process, and called "the proprietary class," or for short, "the proprietors."

The third class distinguished by Quesnay consists mainly of

---

[21] Ibid., p. 88.

those who work on the land—agricultural laborers and capitalist farmers. But agricultural workers are not the only members of the productive class. In addition, "men engaged in fishing ought to be included in the class of those who produce."[22] One should also include in this sector "*the work of the men who are engaged in extracting minerals and metals from the mines.*" [23] Finally, and most surprisingly, "merchants ought to be included in the class of men who produce, provided that they contribute to abundance."[24]

These statements make clear that Quesnay conceived of the productive or agricultural sector more broadly than he is usually given credit for. Commentators have, in general, followed Adam Smith in criticizing Quesnay for regarding manufacturing as sterile and agriculture as the only occupation capable of generating a surplus. From the above passages, though, it seems that foremost in Quesnay's mind was to divide the economy into different sectors based not on the type of employment engaged in, but rather upon whether a surplus was generated or not. All occupations yielding a surplus were called "productive"; all others were denigrated as "sterile". Which occupations are productive and which are sterile then becomes an empirical question. Quesnay's answer, which he derived from the economy of mid-18th century France, was that work on land creates surplus value. Other occupations do not.

Faced with different economic circumstances, such as a surplus-creating industrial sector, Quesnay probably would not have made the assumption that there was something special about agriculture and the regenerative properties of the land, and would have placed manufacturing, along with the labor of the merchant, in the productive sector. Much irrelevant criticism might thus have been avoided. In any event, Quesnay's model is flexible enough to permit the incorporation of a surplus in manufacturing. This surplus in manufacturing would get accumulated by capitalists in the manufacturing sector, would become part of the advances of the sterile class, and would result in further increases in manufactured goods.

Finally, in "Men" Quesnay takes one step closer to the *Tableau* by working out the reproduction process in greater detail. Quesnay writes:

---

[22] Ibid., p. 96.
[23] Ibid., p. 97. The italics here are Quesnay's.
[24] Ibid., p. 97.

The proprietor uses the money he receives from his farmer to purchase the foreign commodities which the merchant has imported; and the merchant returns this money to the farmer who sells him the products yielded by his cultivation. The workers who are paid by the manufacturer, by the husbandman, and by those who employ them, buy produce and commodities for their consumption; and the money is turned back into the cultivation of the land and the production of the manufactured goods which are reproduced.[25]

This passage contains a detailed description of circulation, and also introduces foreign trade into the reproduction process.

As we shall see, circulation here differs from the circulation process in the *Tableau*. In "Men" the proprietors spend *all* their revenue to purchase imported foreign luxuries. In the first version of the *Tableau*, however, Quesnay shows that simple reproduction requires that proprietors spend half their revenues on manufactured goods and half on food produced by the cultivators. Meanwhile, dynamic versions of the *Tableau* demonstrate that if the proprietors spend more than half their revenue on manufactured goods the economy will decline, and will continue to do so until the proprietors' spending propensities change to favor agricultural goods.

A second difference between the reproduction process of "Men" and the reproduction process of the *Tableau* is that in the passage above Quesnay has the proprietor buy *imported* manufactured goods. The reproduction process of the *Tableau*, however, requires that the proprietors purchase manufactured goods produced domestically by the sterile class. In the *Tableau* imported manufacturers are consumed by sterile class workers and used by them in the production of the following year's manufactured goods.

Finally, the money circulation process in "Men" is confusing and inconsistent. Quesnay has money flow from the proprietor to the manufacturing sector and then to the farmer. When the farmer turns the money back into the land, a surplus is again created. The value of this surplus becomes the proprietor's revenue. The problem here is one of timing. According to the passage quoted above, the manufacturer pays his worker after money is returned by the manufacturer to the farmer, who then buys produce and manufactured goods for consumption purposes. Clearly this is an impossibili-

---

[25] Ibid., p. 92f.

ty; for if all money has been returned to the farmer, there is no money left in the coffers of the manufacturer to pay his workers. Despite these problems, the above passage from "Men" is important because of the attempt on Quesnay's part to set forth explicitly the reproduction relations among the three sectors or classes of society.

Quesnay's final *Encyclopedia* article, "Taxation," contains the first statement of the famous Physiocratic doctrine of taxation. As is well-known, the Physiocrats maintained that taxes ought to be placed only on the proprietors. A tax on the farmer, Quesnay argues, would destroy the means of production. It would reduce agricultural sector inputs and hence the output of agricultural goods. This is not true of a tax on the proprietors. Such a tax "would be paid costlessly, and would not be detrimental to the farmer."[26]

These policy prescriptions regarding taxation have the status of mere assertion in "Taxation." This is so because Quesnay had yet to formulate his *Tableau.* Once Quesnay developed a model, the effects of various kinds of taxes could be demonstrated with that model. In later works, Quesnay attempts just such demonstrations. The development of the *Tableau* thus raised the logical status of the Physiocratic doctrine of a unique tax on the proprietors. It was no longer a mere assertion; it became the conclusion of a deductive argument.

SECTION II

Sometime between 1757, when he finished his *Encyclopedia* articles, and December 1758, the publication date of the first edition of the *Tableau,* Quesnay made a major analytical advance. This advance was not the development of some new principle or assumption. Nor was it the modification of the ideas developed in the *Encyclopedia* articles. The ideas and assumptions of the *Tableau* all existed in the *Encyclopedia* articles. What was missing was an integration and formalization of these ideas. The achievement of the *Tableau* was to fill in this missing link. It made Quesnay's assumptions more precise and incorporated them into a whole—a model of the circulation and production processes which demonstrated that the economy could reproduce itself. By illustrating his principles numerically, Quesnay was forced to make more precise relationships

---

[26] Ibid., p. 107.

that might have been left vague or overlooked in a mere prose description. More important, by so doing Quesnay developed the first mathematical model of the economy.

Between December 1758 and December 1759[27] Quesnay published three editions of the *Tableau*. They are all essentially the same in substance; differing only slightly in detail and means of presentation. All three editions contain the famous zig-zag diagram. Along with this, each edition contains an explanation of the diagram and a statement of the principles and assumptions upon which the construction of the diagram is based.

In the first edition, explanatory notes are placed in the margins of the zig-zag diagram, and a set of assumptions under the heading "Remarks on the Variations in the Distribution of the Annual Revenue of a Nation" is appended. The zig-zag diagram of the first edition—reproduced as Figure #2-1—has a base of 400 livres.[28] This base is the value of agricultural advances, which Quesnay assumes is also the value of the agricultural surplus.

Figure #2-1 contains three columns. Different columns represent different sectors of the economy. Within each sector there are at least two classes. The productive sector consists of a class of capitalist farmers and a class of agricultural laborers. The non-producing sector consists of three classes—church, state employees, and landowners. Finally, the manufacturing sector is composed of three classes—a class of self-employed artisans, a class of manufacturing capitalists, and a class of sterile laborers. In each case there is one class which is predominant within the sector. Workers are dominant in the two producing sectors; while proprietors or landowners are the major class within the non-producing sector. For this reason Quesnay often refers to the different sectors in terms of the dominant class, and often calls the sectors "classes." In what follows I will tend to follow Quesnay's terminology. However, it should always be remembered that these so-called classes are in fact different economic sectors.

The column at the left of Figure #2-1 is for the productive

---

[27] The exact publication date of the third edition is unknown. It is generally taken to be some time late in 1759. See "The 1758-9 'Editions' of the *Tableau Économique*" by Ronald L. Meek in Marguerite Kuczynski and Ronald L. Meek, eds. *Quesnay's Tableau Économique* (New York: Augustus M. Kelley, 1972).

[28] Ibid., Appendix A, no page number.

FIGURE #2-1
THE FIRST EDITION OF THE *TABLEAU*

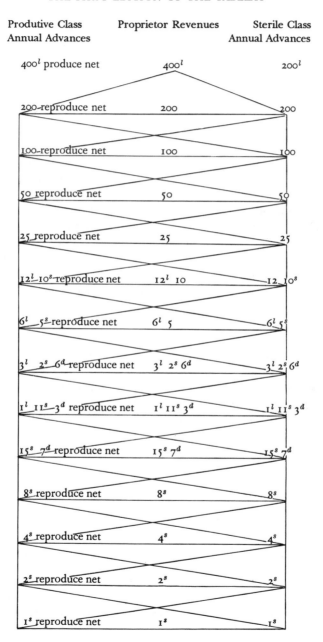

Produtive Class Annual Advances	Proprietor Revenues	Sterile Class Annual Advances
400^l produce net	400^l	200^l
200 reproduce net	200	200
100 reproduce net	100	100
50 reproduce net	50	50
25 reproduce net	25	25
$12^l 10^s$ reproduce net	12^l 10	12 10^s
6^l 5^s reproduce net	6^l 5	$6^l 5^s$
3^l 2^s 6^d reproduce net	$3^l 2^s 6^d$	$3^l 2^s 6^d$
$1^l 11^s 3^d$ reproduce net	$1^l 11^s 3^d$	$1^l 11^s 3^d$
$15^s 7^d$ reproduce net	$15^s 7^d$	$15^s 7^d$
8^s reproduce net	8^s	8^s
4^s reproduce net	4^s	4^s
2^s reproduce net	2^s	2^s
1^s reproduce net	1^s	1^s

sector. At the beginning of the production period it is advanced or given 400 livres. Quesnay does not state whether these advances are money, commodity bundles, or something else entirely. All we are told is that 400 livres of advances produce a net product of 400 livres. Below the figure for advances is a series of numbers. These show the expenditure by other classes on the commodities produced by the productive sector. The expenditures depend upon the money receipts of the other two sectors and the propensity of these sectors to spend money on the commodities produced by the productive class. Expenditures on agricultural goods add up to 400 livres. This is based on the assumption that all classes will spend half of any money receipts on food produced by the productive sector and half on manufactured goods produced by the sterile sector.

The column at the right is for the manufacturing or sterile class. Manufacturing sector advances are 200 livres. These advances are used to produce manufactured goods. Below this are figures showing the expenditures of other classes on manufactured foods. The circulation process sends 400 livres to the manufacturing sector, which sells 400 livres of manufactured goods.

Finally, the center column shows proprietor revenues and expenditures. Proprietors begin with a revenue of 400 livres, which is the value of the surplus from the previous production period. The revenue is spent half on agricultural goods and half on manufactured goods. Two hundred is thus spend on agricultural goods, putting 200 livres into the hands of farmers. This money they use to purchase inputs, which will reproduce and yield a net product of 200. Proprietors also spend 200 on manufactured goods, putting 200 livres into the hands of artisans. This will be used to purchase inputs and result in the production of 200 manufactured goods, but no net product. In the second stage of the reproduction process, each producing class uses its 200 livres of income to purchase 100 livres of manufactured goods and 100 livres of agricultural goods. Hence each producing class receives another 100 livres, which again is spent half within the class and half on the commodities of the other producing class. This process continues with expenditures and receipts getting smaller and smaller at each stage. At the very end of the entire circulation process 400 livres is sent to each producing class. These are the column sums of the productive and manufacturing classes.

The 400 livres received by the productive class are used to pay the proprietors their revenues. Circulation sends 400 livres to the sterile class. But here only "200 livres have to be kept back for the annual advances. Two hundred livres remain for expenditure."[29] Where the 200 livres is spent, or on what, Quesnay is silent. Quesnay also seems to ignore the fact that while the sterile class receives 400 livres it has also spent half this sum on agricultural goods. At the end of the circulation process depicted by the zig-zags, the sterile class has only 200 livres. A similar point holds for the agricultural class, which also spends half its 400 livres in receipts and so will only have 200 livres in its possession when the circulation process represented by the zig-zags have been completed.

Quesnay's marginal notes at the left of the *Tableau* contain a few assumptions about population and per capita consumption. These assumptions play an important role in the mechanics of the *Tableau*. According to Quesnay, the proprietor's revenue of 400 livres enables the proprietor to purchase the food and manufactured goods on which he will live. But the proprietor's expenditures—200 livres on agricultural goods and 200 livres on manufactured goods— can support one person in each of the producing classes. So while proprietors live on 400 livres, workers in the manufacturing and agricultural sectors subsist on 200 livres apiece. Per capita consumption of the proprietors is therefore twice the per capita consumption of the producing classes.

A set of "Remarks" also accompany the zig-zag diagram. These provide the overarching assumptions upon which the construction and operation of the table are based. There is substantial repetition and overlap in Quesnay's remarks, but they can be broken down into several broad categories.

(1)   *No Savings.* This proposition is expressed in Remarks 1, 5, and 6. The theme running through these three remarks is that "the whole of the 400 millions of revenue enters into the annual circulation and runs through it to the full extent of its course; and that it is never formed into monetary fortunes, which check the flow of a part of this annual revenue of a nation...to the detriment of the reproduction of this revenue and the well-being of the people."[30] This holds true especially with respect to the proprietors[31] and the taxes collected by the govern-

---

[29] Meek, *Economics of Physiocracy*, p. 111.
[30] Ibid., p. 109. The quotation is from Remark #1.
[31] Ibid., p. 112 (Remark #5).

ment.[32]

(2) *Balanced Foreign Trade.* Remarks 2, 3, 4, and 10 all stipulate that the trade account of the economy must be in balance. Moreover, a nation should not lose its wealth by the "desertion of inhabitants who take their wealth out of the kingdom."[33] Most interesting is Remark #4, where Quesnay expresses his opposition to the mercantilist position that export surpluses or the influx of specie is associated with the increased wealth of a nation. Rather, Quesnay maintains the loss often falls on that nation receiving additional money. Quesnay fails to explain or defend this positions, but it is not hard to discern why export surpluses should result in economic decline. Production for Quesnay occurs by using commodities rather than by factors of production. This is the economic function of advances in the *Tableau.* When more goods are exported, less are available for production and so output must fall. To prevent this from occurring, export surpluses must be prohibited, or balanced trade assumed.

(3) *No Government Interference or Disturbance of the Economy.* There are a number of ways that government actions can ruin an economy. Taxes can be too high. They can also be placed on the cultivators of the land rather than on proprietor revenues. This increases the costs of tax collection, and destroys the advances necessary for agricultural production and the creation of a net product. Improper taxation also hinders trade.[34] Quesnay also warns the government not to interfere with expenditure; not to make loans which result in the formation of rentier incomes; and not to expand its expenditures beyond those necessary for the prosperity of the nation. Finally, the government should not be concerned with increasing the population of a nation.[35]

(4) *Modern Agricultural Techniques are Employed.* This requires increased use of livestock in farming[36] and

---

[32] Meek, *Economics*, p. 112. (Remark #6).
[33] Ibid., p. 112. (Remark #10).
[34] Ibid., p. 112. (Remark #7).
[35] Ibid., p. 113 (Remarks #17, #19, #21, and #22).
[36] Ibid., p. 113. (Remark #15).

sufficient original advances.[37] This assumption is important because modern agricultural techniques are necessary if agricultural advances are to produce a net product equal to the value of advances in agriculture. If agricultural advances do not reproduce 100%, the net product, proprietor revenues, and the demand for produced commodities all fall. This causes the economy to decline. In contrast, if agricultural advances reproduce by more than 100%, net product, proprietor revenues and demand all increase, and the economy grows. The static equilibrium depicted in the first edition of the *Tableau* thus requires that agricultural advances reproduce exactly 100%.

(5) *A High Price for Agricultural Goods.* As we shall see, Quesnay really had no theory of price or value. Nonetheless, he believed high agricultural prices are advantageous because they encourage cultivation of the land. High agricultural prices are also desirable when trading with a foreign nation. The higher the price of agricultural goods, the more manufactured goods a given quantity of food will fetch. It is important though that the high price of agricultural goods not unduly reduce the well-being of laborers. For if workers cannot afford to consume a sufficient quantity of food, their productivity will fall. Consequently, the revenue of the nation and annual reproduction will also fall.[38]

(6) *Encouragement is Given to Production Rather than to Luxury Consumption.* This is the essence of Remarks #16 and #17. In these remarks, Quesnay is making two related points. First, commodities should be employed in the production of other commodities rather than being used for non-productive consumption. Only if commodities are used as a means of subsistence for workers engaged in production will total production increase. Quesnay's second point is that consumption should be of agricultural rather than of manufactured goods. Although the first edition of the *Tableau* provides neither a statement nor an analysis of the consequence of excess con-

---

[37] Ibid., p. 112 (Remark #8).
[38] Ibid., p. 113 (Remark #14).

sumption of manufactured goods, as the author of "Corn" Quesnay surely understood the benefits of increased production and consumption of agricultural goods. Later *Tableaux* demonstrate the economic decline that results from violating this assumption.

(7)   *No Attempt is Made to Create Prosperity by Credit.* The issuing of credit leads to usurious gains. These gains, in turn, come to be preferred to the gains to be made by agriculture. Production declines as individuals attempt to make money by lending money. The construction of the *Tableau* assumes to the contrary that individuals are engaged in productive enterprises.[39]

(8)   *The Nation Can Expand Its Agricultural Sector.* It must have sufficient number of agricultural workers and enough land to cultivate.[40] This assumption is important because the *Tableau* is not an actual representation of the French economy. Instead it portrays reproduction relations that would occur if all the Physiocratic reforms were put into effect. One consequence of these reforms would be a dramatic increase in output. Such an increase, though, would not be possible unless more land were available and the nation had a sufficient number of agricultural laborers.

Edition two of the *Tableau* differs minimally from the first edition. The main change is that all figures for advances and revenues are increased by 50%. The base of the second edition thus becomes 600 rather than 400 livres. Quesnay thought these changes were necessary to make the *Tableau* more realistic.[41] Appended to the second edition is a set of maxims under the heading "Extract from the Royal Economic Maxims of M. de Sully,"[42] which are substantially identical to the "Remarks" of the first edition.

The third edition of the *Tableau* consists of three components:

---

[39] Ibid., p. 113. (Remarks #18 and #19).

[40] These are Remarks #9 and #20, Ibid., pp. 112 and 113 respectively.

[41] Ibid., p. 117.

[42] Sully was "the favorite minister, chief agent, and almost sole advisor of the most popular monarch [Henri IV] who ever sat on the throne of France" according to Henry Higgs, *The Physiocrats* (London: MacMillan & Co., 1897), p. 31. Higgs also contends that the maxims were not Sully's, and that the Physiocrats attempted to take advantage of the similarities between their principles and those of Sully in addition to taking advantage of Sully's good name.

a zig-zag diagram, a set of explanatory notes entitled "Explanation of the *Tableau Économique*" and again the "Extract from the Royal Economic Maxims of M. de Sully." The zig-zag diagram of the third edition— reproduced as Figure #2-2— has a base of 600 livres. All marginal notes have been removed. These become, in part, the explanatory notes of the third edition. The other part of the "Explanation" is a number of new principles and analytic advances.

Sometime between publication of the second and third editions of the *Tableau* Quesnay recognized the possibility of using the *Tableau* to show economic growth and economic decline. The third edition presents only a static *Tableau*, where 600 livres manufactured goods and 1200 livres agricultural goods are produced every year. However, Quesnay does describe the workings of a dynamic *Tableau* and he does calculate the resulting changes in revenues, output, and advances. The case Quesnay considers is one in which the consumption of luxury manufactured goods increases by one-sixth.[43] In the static *Tableau* it was assumed that all classes spend half their income on manufactured goods and half on agricultural goods. Now the consumption of manufactured goods increases by one-sixth, to 7/12 of income. Correspondingly, the consumption of agricultural goods falls by one-sixth, to 5/12 of income. The effect of these changes is to reduce the revenue reproduced from 600 livres to 400 livres. On the other hand, if the propensity to consume agricultural goods increases to 7/12 and the propensity to consume manufactured goods decreases to 5/12, the revenue reproduced would increase from 600 to 800 livres.[44] In addition, Quesnay identifies a number of differ-

---

[43] In dynamic versions of the *Tableau* it is the consumption of luxury manufactured goods that is supposed to cause economic decline. The real issue, however, is not luxury consumption versus the consumption of necessities, but consumption of goods produced in the surplus-generating sector versus consumption of goods produced the sterile sector. Since the proprietor's per capita consumption of agricultural goods is twice that of the producing classes they must consume luxury agricultural goods—i.e., agricultural goods over what is necessary for subsistence—as well as luxury manufactured goods.

[44] Kuczynski and Meek, *Quesnay's Tableau Economique*, p. ii. Quesnay's calculations of the changes in revenue are incorrect. The sector on which 7/12 of incomes are spent will experience an increase in demand, and its column total will increase to 655. The sector on which 5/12 of incomes are spent will experience a reduction in demand. Its column total will fall to 513. Hence revenues will increase to 655 when 7/12 is spent on agricultural goods and will decrease to 513 when 5/12 of income is spent on agricultural goods. For an explanation of how these figures were derived see Chapter IV.

FIGURE #2-2

THE THIRD EDITION OF THE *TABLEAU*

PRODUCTIVE CLASS	PROPRIETORS	STERILE CLASS

Annual advances required to produce a revenue of 600^l are 600^l	Annual revenue	Annual advances for the works of sterile expenditure are

600^l produce net ·········· 600^l 300^l

Products *one-half goes here* ············ *one-half goes here*   Works, etc.

300^l reproduce net ···· *one-half* ····· 300^l *one-half goes here* ···· 300^l

goes here

150 reproduce net ·········· 150   *one-half, etc.* ···· 150

one-half, etc.

75 reproduce net ·········· 75   75

37··10^s reproduce net ·········· 37··10   37··10

18··15 reproduce net ·········· 18··15   18··15

9··· 7 ··· 6^d reproduce net ·······9··· 7··· 6^d 9··· 7··· 6^d

4··13 ··· 9 reproduce net ········4··13··· 9   4··13··· 9

2··· 6··10 reproduce net ········2···6··10   2···6··10

1··· 3 ··· 5 reproduce net ·······1··· 3 ··· 5   1··· 3··· 5

0··11 ··· 8 reproduce net ·······0··11··· 8   0··11··· 8

0··· 5 ·· 10 reproduce net ·······0··· 5··10   0··· 5··10

0 ··· 2··11 reproduce net ·······0··· 2··11   0··· 2··11

0 ··· 1 ··· 5 reproduce net ·······0··· 1··· 5   0··· 1··· 5

etc.

ent factors that would likewise lead to economic decline. These factors are:[45]

   (i)   a tax system encroaching on agricultural advances

   (ii)   a tax system subject to high costs of collection

   (iii) excess expenditure on litigation

   (iv) lack of freedom to export agricultural goods

   (v)   lack of freedom in internal trade

   (vi) harassment of the inhabitants of the countryside by the sovereign

   (vii) failure of the monies paid as rent to the proprietors to return to the agricultural sector.

In all cases Quesnay fails to describe how and why the economy declines for the stated reason. More importantly, in no case are we provided with a *Tableau* showing the economic decline that results.

A further advance made in the third edition of the *Tableau* is Quesnay's more detailed description of the reproduction process that is depicted by the zig-zags. In this edition of the *Tableau*, 1200 livres of agricultural goods are produced. This output is distributed as follows. Three hundred livres are bought by the proprietors. Another 300 livres is purchased by the manufacturing class, "of which one-half, amounting to 150 livres, is consumed for subsistence within this class, and the other half, amounting to 150 livres is taken for external trade."[46] Quesnay recognized the importance of balanced trade in the first two editions of the *Tableau*, and cited the necessity of free trade in his *Encyclopedia* articles. But only in the third edition of the *Tableau* does Quesnay recognize that foreign traded must be an integral part of the *Tableau*'s reproduction process. Moreover, as we shall see in the next chapter, Quesnay has precisely and correctly calculated that 150 livres of agricultural goods must be exported in exchange for 150 livres of manufactured imports. Finally, the remaining 600 livres of the 1200 livres of agricultural goods produced are used within the agricultural sector to feed men and maintain livestock.

Unfortunately, there is a serious error in these computations. Quesnay's mistake can be demonstrated in two ways. First, according to the zig-zag diagram, total agricultural receipts add up to 600

---

[45] Ibid., p. xi-xii.
[46] Ibid., p. iii.

livres. By assumption, half of all receipts are spent within the agricultural sector and half are spent on manufactured goods. Agricultural sector purchases of agricultural goods must then be only 300 livres, rather than the 600 livres claimed by Quesnay. Second, by assumption the advances of the manufacturing sector are only half of manufacturing sector receipts. Where the other half of these receipts go is left unexplained. In principle, it can go to buy only agricultural or manufactured goods, since the proprietors produce no commodities. But according to the *Tableau*, the sterile class sells its entire output of manufactured goods to the proprietors and the productive class. Three hundred is sold to the proprietors and another 300 gets sold to the agricultural sector when the zig-zags work their way through the economy. Only agricultural goods remain as a source of expenditure for the other half of manufacturing sector receipts. If this is so, the manufacturing sector buys 600 rather than 300 livres of agricultural goods. Only 300 livres of agricultural goods remain for consumption by the agricultural class.

Finally, in the third edition of the *Tableau* Quesnay calculates for the first time the amount of money required for simple reproduction. The supply of money should be approximately the same as the net product. If the supply of money is greater than the net product, the extra money would be of no use and would be exchanged abroad for other goods yielding more satisfaction than holding money.[47] The reverse case, where the supply of money is less than the net product, Quesnay unfortunately says nothing about. In this instance two things might, in principle, happen. The shortage of money may cause economic decline. Decline can result either from reduced expenditures by the proprietors, since with less money in the economy they receive less revenues, or decline can be the consequence of selling commodities abroad in order to obtain the additional money needed. This reduces inputs, and so fewer commodities can be produced. On the other hand, the lack of money may not affect output. Instead, the existing supply of money may be used more intensively; that is, the velocity of circulation may increase. Since Quesnay did not list the shortage of money as one of the causes of decline in the third edition, it would seem as though Quesnay was leaning toward the latter possibility and thought that a shortage of money would cause its velocity to increase. In fact, in

---

[47] Ibid., p. x.

later works—notably "The Second Economic Problem"—Quesnay has the velocity of money increase when the net product outstrips the existing money supply.

SECTION III

The year 1759 also saw the publication of a new edition of *L'Ami des Hommes*. This edition of *L'Ami des Hommes* marked the first time that the *Tableau* was made available to the general public. The first three editions of the *Tableau* were shown to only a few of Quesnay's friends and colleagues, and few copies were printed.

Originally written by Mirabeau, the 1759 edition proclaims joint authorship. Both Quesnay and Mirabeau take credit for the work. The main additions to the 1759 edition are several zig-zag *Tableaux* and an entirely new part dealing with the causes of economic decline. Probably both came from Quesnay's pen. However, even if they were written by Mirabeau, the intellectual contribution of Quesnay had to be extensive. For in 1759 Mirabeau was still having great difficulty deciphering the zig-zags of the *Tableau*.[48]

The *Tableaux* of *L'Ami des Hommes* are not part of the body of the work. Rather, they are interspersed throughout the five volumes with no discussion or explanation at the point at which they appear. Only the newly added part IV discusses the mechanics of the *Tableau* and cites reasons for economic decline.

Six *Tableaux* appear in *L'Ami des Hommes*. The first two are static *Tableaux* virtually identical to the *Tableaux* of the first three editions. A *Tableau* in Volume I contains a base of 600; and a *Tableau* in Volume II contains a base of 1050. Quesnay next provides a dynamic *Tableau* for our inspection. This *Tableau* shows the effects of the excessive consumption of luxury goods. Quesnay assumes that each class spends approximately 3/5 of income receipts on manufactured goods and approximately 2/5 on agricultural goods. Given Quesnay's figures, the propensity to consume agricultural goods is actually .4167 and the propensity to consume manufactured goods is .5833. The proprietors begin with a revenue of 1050 livres, and spend 612.5 livres on manufactured goods and 437.5 livres on food. This gives the manufacturing sector an income of 612.5, of

---

[48] See Meek's translation of the letter from Quesnay to Mirabeau (which must have been written in early 1759) in Meek, *Economics of Physiocracy*, p. 115f.

which 41.67%, or 255.2 is spent on agricultural goods. Similarly, the agricultural sector receives 437.5 and spends 58.33%, or 255.2, on manufactured goods. As usual, income leads to expenditure, which in turn generates more income and more spending. The entire process is depicted in Figure #2-3.[49]

FIGURE # 2-3

TABLEAU SHOWING THE EFFECTS OF EXCESSIVE CONSUMPTION
CONSUMPTION OF MANUFACTURED GOODS

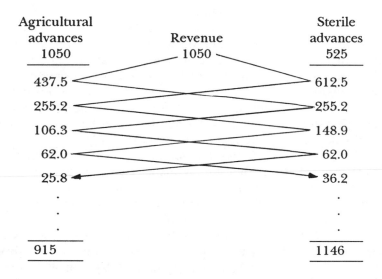

Agricultural output declines as a consequence of the reduced demand for agricultural goods. In the next production period agricultural advances and proprietor revenues both fall to 915 livres. Unanswered by Quesnay, however, is *why* production declines. Moreover, it is unclear from Figure #2-3 how production enters into the *Tableau*. The diagram makes clear the circulation process, but the production process and the relationship between the production process and the circulation process remains an enigma. Chapter IV will attempt to clarify these issues.

---

[49] Victor de Riquetti, Marquis de Mirabeau and Francois Quesnay, *L'Ami des Hommes* (Avignon, 1762), Vol. II, p. 66.

The fourth *Tableau* in *L'Ami des Hommes* shows the effects of the *spoliation* of agricultural advances.[50] Advances can become spoiled as a result of taxation, or, from natural calamities and catastrophes. This leaves fewer inputs to use in production, and as a consequence output, the net product, and proprietor revenues are reduced. Lower proprietor revenues will reduce the demand for agricultural goods in the next production period. It will also reduce the total demand for manufactured goods in succeeding periods. Manufacturing output, and hence the advances of the manufacturing class, will also decline.

Quesnay next employs the *Tableau* to analyze the effects of reduced productivity in agriculture.[51] When productivity falls, the net product is reduced. Quesnay's *Tableau* shows a reduction in net product from 600 livres to 120 livres, but not what happens in the next period as a consequence of the fall in proprietor revenues due to the lower net product. It is not hard to extend Quesnay's analysis though. The reduction in proprietor revenues to 120 livres reduces demand for both agricultural and manufactured goods. Output and advances decline in both producing sectors. And with smaller advances and low productivity, proprietor revenues should fall again. In fact, as long as agricultural advances fail to double, proprietor revenues must fall; and they will continue to fall, bringing down with them demand, advances, and production.

The final *Tableau* in *L'Ami des Hommes* demonstrates the effects of an indirect tax of 400 livres on the advances of the productive class. Figure #2-4 shows the destructive effects of such a tax.[52] Agricultural advances and agricultural output both fall. This will affect the net product, and so proprietor revenues, demand, and output will fall in the next period. Output and advances in the manufacturing sector also seem to fall. But Quesnay is not totally clear on this point. On the one hand, demand has increased for manufactured goods because all taxes are spent on manufactured goods. This should increase the output of manufactured goods. On the other hand, advances in manufacturing are always one-half the output of manufactured goods. Starting with advances of 500, output should have been 1000 before the imposition of the indirect tax on

---

[50] Ibid., Vol. IV, p. 77.
[51] Ibid., Vol. V, p. 84. This would be a consequence of increased use of *petite culture*, or small-scale farming.
[52] Ibid., Vol. V, p. 118.

FIGURE #2-4

THE EFFECT OF INDIRECT TAXATION

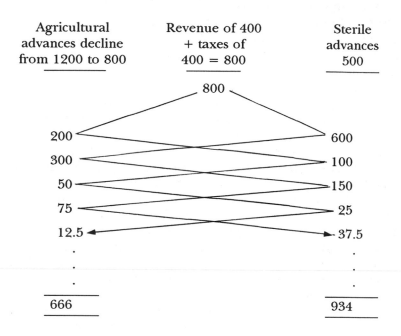

Agricultural advances decline from 1200 to 800	Revenue of 400 + taxes of 400 = 800	Sterile advances 500

agricultural advances. This being the case, the indirect tax seems to have caused manufacturing output to fall from 1000 to 934 livres.

Quesnay's analyses of taxation have always been very confused, and *Tableaux* demonstrating the effects of indirect taxation invariably contain several highly questionable assumptions. In Figure #2-4, for example, Quesnay starts his analysis with a net product (400) that is only of one-third agricultural advances (1200). This low agricultural productivity may be itself be the cause of economic decline. Consequently, the effect of the indirect tax is *not* clear in this case. It may have no effect, or it may contribute to an already deteriorating situation. In addition, Quesnay has the sovereign spend all the new tax receipts exclusively on manufactured goods. They buy no additional food for subsistence. Had half the sovereign's tax receipts been spent on agricultural goods, in accord with Quesnay's usual assumptions regarding consumption, column totals for both producing classes would be 800. The 800 received by the agricultural sector would constitute its advances in the next production period. So without Quesnay's restrictive assumption we would get a once-and-for-all decline in production, but not the continual decline Quesnay argues would result from indirect taxes. Chapter VI will examine the Physiocratic view of taxation in more detail.

In addition to the six *Tableaux*, part VI of *L'Ami des Hommes* contains an analysis and explanation of several possible causes of economic decline. Quesnay identifies six such factors. Three of these—excess consumption of luxury manufactured goods, spoliation, and destructive taxes—were the subject of individual *Tableaux*. The fourth cause of decline is savings. Quesnay argues, contrary to the mercantilists, that money does not contribute to the wealth of nations. It does so only if it is spent. Money that is accumulated impoverishes a nation.[53] Nowhere in *L'Ami des Hommes* does Quesnay provide either a *Tableau* or a numerical example showing the effects of various levels of savings on production, advances, and revenues. Chapter VI will present such a *Tableau* and further analyze the relationships between saving and economic decline. The final two causes of decline are lack of free trade and inadequate contracts for farmers. Both are important because of their effect on prices. Free trade and government contracts for the farmer keep prices high. Restrictions on trade and contracts which keep prices low lead to economic decline. Again, no *Tableaux* are offered showing the malevolent effects of low prices. Nor does Quesnay explain precisely how low prices lead to economic decline. Finally, Quesnay fails to describe how the *Tableau* can be used to distinguish the real from the nominal effects of a price change. If high prices increase real output, the *Tableau*'s columns must show increases in physical output as well as price increases. In a later work, "The First Economic Problem," Quesnay explains his views on price changes in more detail and offers a *Tableau* demonstrating that real output increases with increases in prices. This issue will be examined in greater detail in Chapter VI, after we have come to understand the

---

[53] Ibid., Vol. V, p. 93.

workings of both the static and the dynamic *Tableau*.

Another turning point in the development of the *Tableau* was reached with the publication of *Philosophie Rurale* in 1764. This work contains many *Tableaux*, as well as additional explanations and observations concerning its mechanisms. But perhaps what is most important are the changes in Quesnay's presentation of the *Tableau*. Gone are the zig-zags over which Mirabeau and others, had struggled for so long. In their place is a summary or précis of the distribution process that is depicted in the *Tableau*. Figure #2-5 shows this new method of presenting the *Tableau*.[54]

FIGURE #2-5

PRECIS OF THE *TABLEAU*

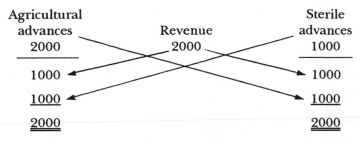

A minor change has been the elimination of the zig-zag transactions and their replacement with one transaction which is equivalent to all previous zig-zags. The zig-zags represent two streams of expenditures. One is a series of expenditures by the agricultural class on manufactured goods. Summing up this series we derive single number showing total purchases of manufactured goods by the agricultural sector. The other series shows manufacturing sector purchases of food. This too can be summed and expressed as a single number. Performing such summations, the *Tableau* is considerably shortened and simplified. Instead of a series of complex criss-crossing lines, the précis sums up these transactions with two lines—a single line starting from agricultural advances and going to purchase 1000 livres of manufactured good, and another line starting from sterile advances and going to purchase 1000 livres of agricultural goods.

---

[54] Francois Quesnay, *Philosophie Rurale* (Amsterdam: Chez Les Libraires Associes, 1764), Vol. I, p. 104.

More substantive changes occur in Quesnay's description of the circulation process of the *Tableau,* and in his assumption that advances reproduce 100%. In the précis it is advances rather than money incomes that seem to determine expenditure. Dropping the assumption that advances reproduce 100% allows the *Tableau* to depict changes in agricultural productivity, and to represent reproduction in impoverished as well as thriving economies. Quesnay observes that when advances reproduce 100% "the revenue is equal to the advances of the productive class," so it is irrelevant to the details of the distribution of productive class expenditures whether we employ revenue or advances. But since "it is simpler and less burdensome to trace the circulation of expenditures in the *Tableau* through revenue than through advances we have preferred it, while understanding that it is advances employed as expenses."[55] Quesnay's point is that when advances reproduce 100% one can present the *Tableau* either with zig-zags, representing expenditures as a function of a sales receipts; or one can represent expenditures as a function of advances. The figures we get in each case are the same, and the results of the respective methods are the same. The two methods are equivalent.

FIGURE #2-6

THE *TABLEAU* WHEN ADVANCES REPRODUCE 50%

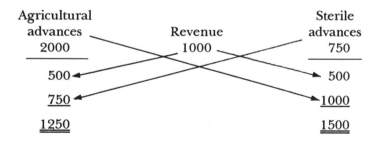

However, when advances do not reproduce 100%, advances are not equal to revenues. The respective methods of determining producing class expenditures are not reducible to one another. For

---

[55] Mirabeau and Quesnay, *L'Ami des Hommes,* p. Vol. II, p. 150-51. The translation here is my own.

example, consider Figure #2-6, where agricultural advances reproduce only 50%.[56] Advances of 2000 create a surplus of only 1000, which is paid to the proprietors as revenue. In this case though it is not the money receipts of the producing classes that determine how much they spend with one another. If receipts determined expenditures, the agricultural sector would buy 500 manufactured goods and the manufacturing sector would buy 500 food. Rather, it is advances that are important in Figure #2-6, and advances that determine expenditures by the producing classes. This is why Quesnay has drawn lines starting from advances.

FIGURE #2-7

THE *TABLEAU* WHEN ADVANCES REPRODUCE 150%

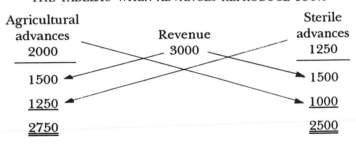

On the other hand, when advances reproduce more than 100%, receipts and sterile advances increase. Figure #2-7 shows the distribution process of a *Tableau* in which advances reproduce 150%.[57] Again, it is advances and *not* revenues that determine expenditure by the producing sectors.

The additional flexibility that results from allowing for changes in agricultural productivity, has required changes in several of the *Tableau*'s relationships. There will be a new relationship between the receipts of the agricultural sector and the output of the agricultural sector. When advances reproduce 100%, agricultural output is twice agricultural receipts, and it is a relatively simple matter to calculate agricultural output from receipts. This relation depended upon the fact that sterile advances were half agricultural receipts. In general though, agricultural output will depend upon two variables: agricultural productivity and inputs of commodities that are used in

---

[56] This *Tableau* appears in *L'Ami des Hommes*, Vol. II, p. 149.
[57] This *Tableau* appears in *L'Ami des Hommes*, Vol. II, p. 157.

producing agricultural goods. Available inputs, in turn, depend on prior output and sales.[58] Output not sold is available to be used in the production of next period's output.

Quesnay employs the précis to demonstrate the effect of indirect taxes, the effect of high prices, and the effect of excess consumption of luxury goods.

Two sets of *Tableaux* are used to demonstrate that indirect taxes result in economic decline. Each set consists of one *Tableau* showing economic decline as a consequence of the imposition of an indirect tax, and another *Tableau* demonstrating that whenever the sovereign returns tax monies, the economy returns to a healthy state. Figure #2-8 shows the decline resulting from an indirect tax of 175 million livres.[59]

Quesnay begins with the assumption that agricultural advances reproduce 150%. Agricultural advances of 630 yield a revenue for the proprietors of 945. Sterile advances of 394 continue to be reproduced without the creation of a surplus. Before imposition of a tax on the two producing classes, the manufacturing sector produced 788 of manufactured goods. 473 was purchased by the proprietors and 315 by the agricultural sector. In turn, the manufacturing class bought and traded for the 788 worth of inputs it would need for the next production period. Before the tax was imposed the agricultural sector produced 1575 worth of agricultural goods, of

---

[58] In general, where Y = agricultural output, AR = agricultural receipts, and SA = sterile advances:

Y = agricultural productivity X 2(Y-(AR + SA)).   (1)

Agricultural output is sold through the *Tableau*'s exchanges, and outside the *Tableau* half the sterile sector receipts, which equals sterile sector advances, goes to buy agricultural goods. Agricultural goods not sold to other classes remain to serve as inputs in next year's production. Thus, agricultural inputs are Y -(AR + SA). Since agriculture employs equal amounts of manufactured and agricultural goods as inputs, total inputs in agriculture will be 2(Y - (AR + SA)). Agricultural output will be this figure times productivity in the agricultural sector. When SA = 1/2(AR), and agricultural productivity = 2-- i.e., when output is twice inputs-- equation (1) reduces to Y = AR. We do not get a simple result when SA is not one-half AR. When advances reproduce 50%, Y = 1.5(AR + SA), which is the solution of Figure #2-5. And when advances reproduce 150%, Y = 1.25 (AR + SA), which is the solution of Figure #2-6.

[59] This *Tableau* appears in *L'Ami des Hommes*, Vol. I, p. 348. A similar *Tableau* appears in *L'Ami des Hommes*, Vol. II, p. 270. The latter *Tableau* has a base of 2000 rather than 945; advances in agriculture reproduce 100% rather than 150%; and the tax imposed is 50 livres rather than 175 livres.

FIGURE #2-8

PRECIS OF THE *TABLEAU* SHOWING THE EFFECTS
OF INDIRECT TAXATION

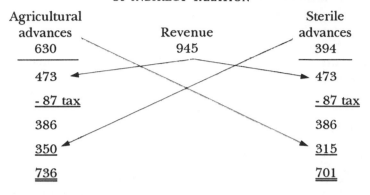

Agricultural advances 630	Revenue 945	Sterile advances 394
473		473
- 87 tax		- 87 tax
386		386
350		315
736		701

which 788 was sold to the sterile class and 472.5 was sold to the proprietors.   This left 314.5 agricultural goods, plus the 315 of purchased manufactured goods, to use for next year's production.

Now let us consider the imposition of an indirect tax on both producing classes. Quesnay assumes a 175 tax is imposed, and that it falls evenly on each producing class. Each producing class then pays 87 to the sovereign. In the sterile sector, the tax reduces inputs, since less money is available to purchase agricultural goods. With 87 fewer inputs, 87 less output gets produced; the reduction being equal to the tax on the sterile sector. Correspondingly, sterile advances fall to 350.5.

The fall in manufacturing sector output reduces manufacturing sector demand for agricultural goods from 788 to 701. 473 worth of agricultural goods is still sold to the proprietors.   The reduced demand for agricultural goods reduces agricultural output. Quesnay calculates the reduction to be the entire amount of the tax (175 livres), however he offers no explanation for this. The reduction in output is a reduction in the net product, which is ultimately borne by the proprietors.

Decline is reversed when the indirect taxes collected by the sovereign are returned. Figure #2-9 demonstrates this situation.[60] It shows that a full tax rebate to both producing sectors returns manufacturing output to 788, and returns sterile advances to 394.

---

[60] Quesnay, *Philosophie Rurale*, Vol. I, p. 350.

Agricultural output is again 1575, and proprietor revenues return to 945 because the surplus increases as a consequence of the tax refund.

FIGURE #2-9

PRÉCIS OF THE *TABLEAU* SHOWING THE EFFECTS
OF RETURNING INDIRECT TAXES

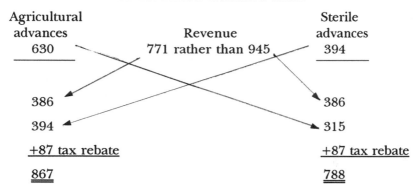

Agricultural advances	Revenue	Sterile advances
630	771 rather than 945	394
386		386
394		315
+87 tax rebate		+87 tax rebate
867		788

To analyze the effect of high prices on the economy Quesnay employs a *Tableau* in which prices increase by one-sixth. The consequences of this are shown in Figure #2-10.[61]

FIGURE #2-10

PRECIS OF THE *TABLEAU* SHOWING THE EFFECTS
OF A PRICE INCREASE

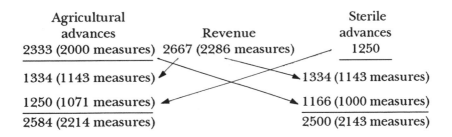

Agricultural advances	Revenue	Sterile advances
2333 (2000 measures)	2667 (2286 measures)	1250
1334 (1143 measures)		1334 (1143 measures)
1250 (1071 measures)		1166 (1000 measures)
2584 (2214 measures)		2500 (2143 measures)

Quesnay starts by assuming that each measure or unit of output sells for 1 livre. Proprietor revenues are 3000 livres, and advances

---

[61] Ibid., Vol. II, p. 166.

of 2000 livres reproduce 150%. Manufacturing output is 2500 measures and agricultural output is 5000 measures. Prices then increase by one-sixth. As a result, the value of agricultural advances rises from 2000 to 2333, and the value of proprietor rents falls from 3000 to 2667 because of the increased price of agricultural advances. Real advances in agriculture do not fall when prices increase-- they remain 2000 measures. Quesnay is not clear about why proprietor rents should fall in this case. If rents represent the value of the agricultural surplus, higher prices for agricultural goods should immediately *increase* proprietor rents. Even if rents increase with a lag (see section II of Chapter VI), proprietor rents should remain constant in the face of higher prices for agricultural goods. In Figure #2-10 Quesnay also has the value of manufacturing sector advances remain unchanged. This facet of the *Tableau* is left unexplained by Quesnay. One might think it is only the price of agricultural goods that rises. However, as is shown in Figure #2-10, when the proprietors purchase manufactured goods, they get only 1143 measures for livres. So manufactured goods *must* have risen in price. Another puzzling feature of Figure #2-10 is that Quesnay maintained that absolute price increases (relative prices remaining unchanged) did not affect quantities. Real output is supposed to be unchanged by the price increase.[62] However, manufacturing sector output, which was 2500 measures, is now just 2143 measures. Agricultural output has fallen also. Initially 5000 measures (2000 for agricultural advances 3000 for proprietor revenues), agricultural output according to Figure #2-10 is only 4286 measures (2000 for agricultural advances and only 2286 for proprietor revenues).

The final application of the *Tableau* in *Philosophie Rurale* is an attempt to show the effects of excess consumption of luxury goods, and the effects of excess consumption of agricultural goods. These *Tableaux* are similar to those in *L'Ami des Hommes*, where Quesnay first demonstrated the effects of excessive consumption of manufactured goods and of switching consumption from manufactured goods to agricultural goods. A major advance in *Philosophie Rurale* is that Quesnay carries the analysis of economic decline beyond one production period. By so doing, he shows that economic decline (and advance) will be continuous. Moreover, Quesnay shows that some of the initial effects of changes in the propensity to consume are only

---

[62] Ibid., Vol. II, p. 165.

temporary. Increased consumption of manufactured goods at the expense of agricultural goods initially raises the output of manufactured goods reduces the output of agricultural goods. These effects are demonstrated in Figure #2-11, [63] where the propensity to consume manufactured goods increases to 3/5, while the propensity to consume agricultural goods falls to 2/5.

FIGURE #2-11

TABLEAU SHOWING ECONOMIC DECLINE AS A RESULT OF INCREASED
CONSUMPTION OF MANUFACTURED GOODS

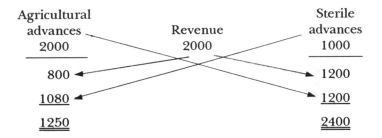

The proprietors spend 800 on agricultural goods and 1200 on manufactured goods. The agricultural class employs a greater proportion of its advances on luxury, manufactured goods. 1200 is spent on manufactured goods, increasing sterile sector receipts. Sterile sector expenditures on agricultural goods also increase. Despite the fact that the zig-zags come from the advances of each producing class rather than from their income receipts, Quesnay here seems to revert back to his position of the three editions of 1758-9 and *L'Ami des Hommes* where incomes rather than advances determine expenditures. According to Figure #2-11, increased expenditure on manufactured goods leads to greater expenditure on food by the sterile class. Manufacturing sector purchases of agricultural goods become 1080 rather than 1000. Moreover, this increase is equal to the increase in sterile receipts times the propensity of the sterile class to spend income on agricultural goods.

From the bottom of Figure #2-11 we see that the output of manufactured goods has increased to 2400, the amount of its sales. Production in the agricultural sector falls from 4000 to 3760. Total

---

[63] Ibid., Vol. IV, p. 32.

output thus increases 40 livres. As a consequence of all this economic activity, sterile advances increase from 1000 to 1200, while
agricultural advances fall from 2000 to 1880. Proprietor revenues
fall proportionately. In the second period, with the propensity to
consume manufactured goods still equal to 3/5, both manufacturing
and agricultural output fall. This result is shown in Figure #2-
12.[64]

FIGURE #2-12

DECLINE IN THE SECOND PRODUCTION PERIOD FROM INCREASED
CONSUMPTION OF MANUFACTURED GOODS

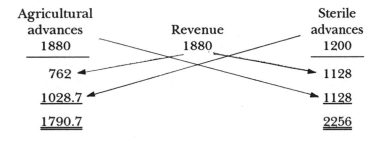

As long as spending propensities do not change, economic
decline will continue unabated. Proprietor revenues will fall,
reducing expenditures on agricultural and manufactured goods. It
is this which causes output to decline in both producing sectors,
leading to further declines in advances, the agricultural surplus, and
proprietor revenues. The process of decline continues unabated as
long as the propensity to consume manufactured goods equals 3/5.
There is no self-adjusting mechanism in the *Tableau*. We get similar
results when the propensity to consume agricultural goods is
increased beyond one-half. In this case agricultural output *increases,*
causing proprietor revenues to rise. Now expenditures on both
agricultural and manufactured goods increase. Output in both
producing sectors increases further. Here, the economy continues
to grow year after year. Again, no self-adjusting mechanism is

---

[64] This *Tableau* is adapted from the one Quesnay provides in *Philosophie Rurale*,
Vol. IV, p. 35. Inexplicably, Quesnay deducts an additional 80 from sterile advances
to get his *Tableau* for the second year. This figure represents increased sterile
purchases of agricultural goods in Figure #2-12. Also, Quesnay adds all additional
receipts to sterile advances, rather than only half of the increase.

postulated.

The publication of the article "Analysis" in the *Journal de L'Agriculture, du Commerce et des Finances* in June 1766 marked another change in Quesnay's presentation of the *Tableau*. In the "Analysis" Quesnay employs a formula of the *Tableau*, a diagram depicting all the exchange relations among the three classes. This allows the reader to more easily follow the circulation process. An additional advantage of the formula is that column totals show the output of each producing sector. This was a property of the original editions of the *Tableau*, and of the *Tableaux* in *L'Ami des Hommes*. In contrast, the précis of *Philosophie Rurale* required several computations before we were able to arrive at a figure for agricultural output. Finally, by clearly showing both production and circulation, the formula makes it easy to infer the input-output relations of the *Tableau*.

The column totals of Figure #2-13 show that the productive class produces 4 milliards of agricultural goods and the sterile class produces 2 milliards of manufactured goods.[65] Of the 4 milliards of agricultural goods that are produced, the proprietors buy 1 milliard. Two milliards of agricultural goods are purchased by the manufacturing class. One milliard is purchased with manufacturing sector advances and another milliard is purchased with the sterile sector's receipts from proprietor expenditures. The final milliard of agricultural output is purchased and used by the agricultural sector itself.

The sterile class produces 2 milliards of manufactured goods. One milliard is purchased by the proprietors and one milliard is purchased by the productive class. This latter purchase is the sum of all zig-zag purchases of agricultural goods by the manufacturing class as depicted in the original versions of the *Tableau*.

Excluded from the formula is the role of foreign trade in the *Tableau*. Also, the formula fails to show the role of money in the *Tableau*. These are points on which all presentations of the *Tableau* falter. It is never clear as we look at various *Tableaux* whether each class has the requisite money to purchase the goods it is supposed to buy. Nor is it clear how the sterile class obtains the necessary manu-

---

[65] Meek, *Economics of Physiocracy*, p. 158. Quesnay's diagram has agricultural output equal to 5 milliards because agricultural expenditures of advances with the agricultural sector is listed as 2 milliards. The additional 1 milliard represents interest goods.

FIGURE #2-13
FORMULA OF THE TABLEAU
Total reproduction: Four milliards

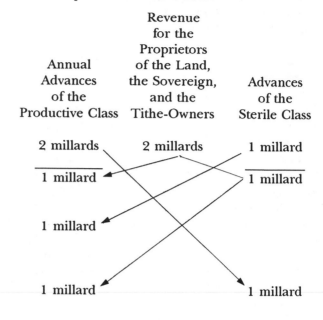

	Annual Advances of the Productive Class	Revenue for the Proprietors of the Land, the Sovereign, and the Tithe-Owners	Advances of the Sterile Class
	2 millards	2 millards	1 millard
Sums which are used to pay the revenue and the interest on the original advances	1 millard		1 millard
	1 millard		
	1 millard		1 millard
Expenditure of the annual advances	1 millard		
Total...	4 millards	Total...	2 millards of which one-half is held back by this class for the following year's advances

factured goods in order to produce more manufactured goods. The sterile class sells its entire output of manufactured goods to the proprietors and to the productive class, thus leaving themselves with no manufactured output. These ambiguities, among others, will be cleared up in Chapter III.

Following publication of "Analysis," Quesnay wrote two articles employing the formula to analyze economic problems. In August of 1766 Quesnay published another article in the *Journal de L'Agricult-*

ure, du Commerce et des Finances. It was entitled "Probleme Economique" and has come to be known as "The First Economic Problem." The purpose of this article was once more to show the effects of a price change using the *Tableau.* In contrast to *Philosophie Rurale*, Quesnay argues here that price increases will result in increased output, and he employs the formula to demonstrate this result. A second article, first published in *Physiocratie*—a collection of Quesnay's writings published by Du Pont de Nemours—is also entitled "Probleme Economique." This article has come to be known as "The Second Economic Problem," and concerns the effect of indirect taxes. Quesnay's intent here, as in *Philosophie Rurale*, was to show the decline that would result from employing such a tax. His analysis was based upon the formula rather than the précis. As we have seen *Tableaux* demonstrating both of these effects, and as we will examine the arguments of these two works in greater detail in Chapter VI, no *Tableaux* from "The First and Second Economic Problems" will be presented here.

Having now surveyed the various versions of the *Tableau*, the changes in Quesnay's presentation, and the uses to which the *Tableau* was put, we next undertake an examination and explanation of the *Tableau* itself. In this endeavor, the ambiguities and problems with the *Tableau* we saw in this chapter will be dealt with. In addition, we shall look at a number of other attempts to make sense of the *Tableau.* Our first undertaking will be to try to understand the static versions of the *Tableau.* This is the task of Chapter III. In Chapter IV we turn our attention to the dynamic versions of the *Tableau.*

CHAPTER III
THE STATIC *TABLEAU*

*I could not ... comprehend these principles in their full
extent, till I had made out a map myself, and withal drawn
up some explanation of that map for my own use.*
—Francois Quesnay[66]

One purpose of Quesnay's *Tableau* was to clearly display
production and distribution relations. This was the object of static
versions of the *Tableau*—those models showing simple reproduction
without growth or decline. Once the static model was elucidated,
Quesnay thought it would be easy to extend the model and examine
the factors causing economic growth and decline. As such, the static
Tableau provided the foundation for Quesnay's dynamic analysis. It
was also the foundation for his economic policy proposals. As
Warren Samuels has pointed out, Physiocracy was essentially "a
theory of how the economy should be organized and controlled."[67]
Starting from a static situation and changing one of the assumptions
of the model while holding everything else constant, the effect of that
change on the economy could be examined and analyzed. Economic
policies could also be argued for or against on the basis of whether
they contributed to economic growth. But such analyses presuppose
an understanding of the workings of the simple, static *Tableau*.

We saw in Chapter II, however, that Quesnay's presentations of
the *Tableau* were far from clear and simple. Confusion concerning
exactly how reproduction takes place in the *Tableau* is the main
reason that for nearly 200 years only Marx and Engels recognized
the importance of the *Tableau*.[68]

Matters changed dramatically with the publication of Ronald

---

[66] Francois Quesnay, *The Economical Table* (New York: Bergman Publishers
1968), p. 12. Spellings have been changed to conform to modern spellings.

[67] Warren J. Samuels, "The Physiocratic Theory of Economic Policy," *Quarterly
Journal of Economics*, 76 (Feb. 1962), 148.

[68] Karl Marx, *Theories of Surplus Value* (Moscow: Foreign Language Publishing
House, 1954), pp. 299-334; Karl Marx, *Capital*, Vol. II (New York: International
Publishers, 1967), pp. 359ff.; and Freidrich Engels, *Herr Eugen Dühring's Revolution
in Science* (New York: International Publishers, no date), p. 276ff.

Meek's essay "Problems of the *Tableau Économique*" in 1960.[69] In this work, Meek attempted to give a clear exposition of the exchange and production relations of the *Tableau* without the use of the famous, yet confusing, zig-zags. Instead, Meek employed a table, with each sector given a column of that table. The commodities held by each sector could then be listed under the appropriate column; and by successive tables, changes in sector holdings, and thus exchange and production, could be represented.

Meek's method of presentation, however, exposes several inconsistencies within the *Tableau*. Unfortunately, Meek does not discuss these problems. Nor does he indicate how we might deal with them. The same holds true of earlier attempts by Shigeto Tsuru[70] and Henri Woog[71] to circumvent the confusing zig-zags.

The reconstructions of Meek, Tsuru, and Woog are presented in Sections I through III of this chapter respectively. Section IV then discusses a recent attempt to explain the workings of the *Tableau* by W.A. Eltis.[72] Eltis, like his precursors, believes this can be done without employing those perplexing zig-zags. Each of these sections includes, in addition, a critique and discussion of the problems with the author's reconstruction. Section V contains a reconstruction of the *Tableau* free of the problems that befall these other attempts, while remaining faithful to Quesnay's actual assumptions. Finally, Section VI attempts to bring together the analysis of this chapter with the different variants and presentations of the static *Tableau* examined in Chapter II.

SECTION I

The following assumptions are needed to reconstruct the *Tableau* as Meek has presented it, and to understand how exchange and production will take place in society:

---

[69] Ronald L. Meek, "Problems of the *Tableau Économique*," *Economica* 27 (Nov. 1960), 322-347. This essay is reprinted in Ronald L. Meek, *The Economics of Physiocracy* (Cambridge: Harvard University Press, 1963), pp. 265-295.

[70] Shigeto Tsuru, "On Reproduction Schemes," Appendix A in Paul Sweezy, *The Theory of Capitalist Development* (New York: Monthly Review Press, 1942), pp. 365-7.

[71] Henri Woog, *The Tableau Économique of François Quesnay* (Switzerland: A Francke A.G. Verlag Bern, 1950).

[72] W. A. Eltis, "François Quesnay: A Reinterpretation 1. The *Tableau Economique*," *Oxford Economic Papers* 27 (July 1975), 167-200.

Class Assumptions

(1) Society is composed of three classes: a productive class of agricultural workers, a class of proprietors or landlords, and a manufacturing class. The productive class produces food and raw materials; the manufacturing class, manufactured goods; and the proprietors produce nothing—at least, nothing of economic significance.

(2) The productive class is the only class which generates a surplus.

(3) The productive class must pay a rent every year to the proprietors. This rent is the price equivalent of the surplus generated by the productive class for the year.

(4) The rent payments received by the proprietors are all used for consumption.

Population Assumption

(5) The proprietors constitute one-quarter of the entire population; the manufacturing class comprises another one-quarter of the population; and the productive class consists of the remaining one-half of the population.

Consumption Assumptions

(6) The per capita consumption for the manufacturing class is equal to the per capita consumption for the productive class, which is equal to one-half of the per capita consumption of the proprietors.

(7) All classes divide their consumption equally between food and manufactured goods. These are the only goods consumed by members of society.

Input-Output Assumptions

(8) The only *explicit* assumption here is that in the productive sector $X of inputs yields $2X worth of outputs. For Quesnay, inputs are commodities rather than factors of production.

Endowments Assumption

(9) Meek begins with a variant of the *Tableau* in which the three classes are in possession of the following holdings:

Productive Class	Proprietors	Manufacturing Class
$1000 money	($2000 in rent claims)	$1000 money
$1000 raw materials		
$3000 food		

Meek next introduces a sequential analysis of production and exchange in eight steps. Step Number One: The manufacturing class buys $1000 raw materials from the productive class. This leads to:

Productive Class	Proprietors	Manufacturing Class
$2000 money	($2000 in rent claims)	$1000 raw materials
$3000 food		

Step Number Two: The productive class pays $2000 money to the proprietors as rent. This eliminates the proprietors' rent claims, and we now have:

Productive Class	Proprietors	Manufacturing Class
$3000 food	$2000 money	$1000 raw materials

Step Number Three: The manufacturing class works up $1000 worth of raw materials into $2000 of manufacturing goods, resulting in:

Productive Class	Proprietors	Manufacturing Class
$3000 food	$2000 money	$2000 mfg'd goods

Step Number Four: The proprietors purchase $1000 food from the productive class and $1000 manufactured goods from the manufacturing class. This will enable the proprietors to consume equal amounts of food and manufactured goods as required by assumption #7. These exchanges also lead to the following position:

Productive Class	Proprietors	Manufacturing Class
$2000 food	$1000 food	$1000 mfg'd goods.
$1000 money	$1000 mfg'd goods	$1000 money

Step Number Five: The manufacturing class buys $1000 food

from the productive class, bringing the situation to:

Productive Class	Proprietors	Manufacturing Class
$1000 food	$1000 food	$1000 mfg'd goods
$2000 money	$1000 mfg'd goods	$1000 food

Step Number Six: The productive class purchases $1000 manufactured goods from the manufacturing class, so that the holdings become:

Productive Class	Proprietors	Manufacturing Class
$1000 food	$1000 food	$1000 money
$1000 money	$1000 mfg'd goods	$1000 food
$1000 mfg'd goods		

Step Number Seven: The manufacturing class exports $500 food and imports $500 manufactured goods. This is needed because by assumptions #5, #6, #7 total food consumption of the manufacturing class must be one-half the total food consumption of the productive class. This is also consistent with Quesnay's explanatory remarks about the role of foreign trade in the *Tableau*. The holdings of each class are now the following:

Productive Class	Proprietors	Manufacturing Class
$1000 food	$1000 food	$ 500 mfg'd goods
$1000 money	$1000 mfg'd goods	$ 500 food
$1000 mfg'd goods		$1000 money

Step Number Eight: All food and manufactured goods are consumed, and production takes place in the productive sector only, resulting in an output of $3000 food and $1000 raw materials. This doubling of advances by the productive class represents the realization of assumption #8. In the manufacturing sector, $500 food and $500 manufactured goods disappear without production taking place. This represents consumption of means of subsistence by the manufacturing class. No production takes place here because production in the manufacturing sector had taken place at Step Number Three. By assumption #3, the proprietors again have $2000 in rent claims. So, we find ourselves back at the original position of holdings:

Productive Class	Proprietors	Manufacturing Class
$1000 money	($2000 in rent claims)	$1000 money

$1000 raw materials
$3000 food

Meek's tabular reconstruction of the *Tableau* clearly shows the circular flow of exchange in society and the commodities that each class produces. It also has the advantage of showing money as well as commodity flows, thus enabling us to ascertain that each class can make the purchases it is supposed to. However, Meek's reconstruction suffers from several defects.

First, at Step Number Three the manufacturing class takes $1000 worth of raw materials and converts them into $2000 of manufactured goods. This appears to be some sort of surplus created by the manufacturing class and, as such, contradicts assumption #2—that only the productive class can generate a surplus. Granted this surplus is later consumed by the manufacturing class (when food and manufactured goods disappear at Step Number Eight). Nonetheless, the manufacturing class has inexplicably increased the value of its holdings at Step Number Three.

Moreover, at Step Number Three, when the workers of the manufacturing class process the $1000 of raw materials and create $2000 worth of manufactured goods, they are paid no wages. Nor do they receive food to sustain themselves while they are working. As the table prior to Step Number Three shows, the manufacturing class has in its possession at this time only the $1000 worth of raw materials which it uses as inputs in the production of $2000 in manufactured goods. So, no wages or food could possibly come into play at Step Number Three. Clearly this is a major problem with the Meek reconstruction.

Finally, it would seem as though manufactured goods should be required (in addition to food and raw materials) in the production of manufactured goods. Manufactured goods, in the form of clothing and housing, will have to be consumed by manufacturing sector workers as part of their subsistence requirements. In addition, tools and machines are necessary to make plows for the productive class and luxury goods for the proprietors, as well as to maintain the tools and machines which the manufacturing class itself uses. So, some manufactured goods must be used by the manufacturing class at Step Number Three. But again, the manufacturing goods must be used by the manufacturing class at Step Number Three. But again, the manufacturing class has no manufactured goods at this point. Even if tools and machinery are implicitly assumed, but do not appear in the *Tableau* itself, there remains the problem that no provision is made for their replacement.[73]

Thus, the Meek reconstruction fails on several accounts.

The above problems stem from one important error on Meek's part. Meek separates production and consumption in manufacturing. If production is to be by means of commodities, then commodities must be consumed as commodities are produced. Production is consumption. If, on the other hand, commodities are produced by factors of production, the relations are separate and distinct. Factors of production produce commodities and then households consume these goods.

Quesnay held that commodities are produced by commodities. Separating production and consumption creates a conflict between this neoclassical assumption and the classical assumptions Quesnay held and incorporated into the *Tableau*. Because Meek separates the processes of production and consumption in the manufacturing sector, raw materials are magically transformed into manufactured goods, and a surplus is created at one stage of the production process. Later this surplus disappears mysteriously.

SECTION II

Prior to Meek's pathbreaking paper, Tsuru's appendix to *The Theory of Capitalist Development* was undoubtedly the best attempt at explaining the *Tableau*'s reproduction scheme. Tsuru's reconstruction employed a diagram, with each class occupying a different quadrant of the diagram. Holdings of each class were shown in its quadrant; and a series of arrows showed commodity and money flows. Unfortunately, Tsuru attempted to show all the exchanges depicted by the *Tableau* on a single diagram. The sequential aspect of the *Tableau*—the fact that some exchanges are prerequisites for other exchanges—gets lost in such a presentation. However, Tsuru's diagram can be expanded into a sequential analysis of the *Tableau*'s exchange relations, and his reconstruction of the *Tableau* set forth along the line of a series of Meekian tables.

Tsuru's reconstruction requires that we make the following assumptions:

---

[73] This point is made by Mark Blaug, *Economic Theory in Retrospect*, 3rd ed. (Cambridge: Cambridge University Press, 1978), p. 28.

(1´) through (4´)-- Class Assumptions are the same as (1) through (4).

(5´) through (8´) *Population Assumption, Consumption Assumptions*, and *Input-Output Assumptions*—No explicit population assumptions are made. Nor are there any explicit assumptions about per capita consumption for each class or about the distribution of consumption between food and manufactured goods. Finally, no explicit input-output assumptions are made. There are, however, important *implicit* assumptions made about population, consumption and input-output relations which are discussed in the critique of Tsuru below.

(9´) *Endowments Assumption*—Contra Quesnay and Meek, the original holdings of the three classes following production by both the manufacturing classes are assumed by Tsuru to be as follows:[74]

Productive Class	Proprietors	Manufacturing Class
$2000 money	($2000 in rent claims)	$2000 mfg'd goods
$3000 food		
$2000 raw materials		

Tsuru then presents six sequential stages of production and exchange. Step #1´: The productive class pays $2000 money to the proprietors as rent, thus eliminating proprietor rent claims:

Productive Class	Proprietors	Manufacturing Class
$3000 food	$2000 money	$2000 mfg'd goods
$2000 raw materials		

Step #2´: The proprietors purchase $1000 food from the productive class and $1000 manufactured goods from the manufacturing class, so that the situation becomes:

Productive Class	Proprietors	Manufacturing Class
$2000 food	$1000 food	$1000 mfg'd goods
$2000 raw materials	$1000 mfg'd goods	$1000 money
$1000 money		

Step #3´: The manufacturing class buys $1000 food from the

---

[74] This is the tabular equivalent of Tsuru's diagram #1, "On Reproduction Schemes," Appendix A in Paul Sweezy, *The Theory of Capitalist Development*, p. 366.

productive class, resulting in:

Productive Class	Proprietors	Manufacturing Class
$1000 food	$1000 food	$1000 mfg'd goods
$2000 raw materials	$1000 mfg'd goods	$1000 food
$2000 money		

Step #4´: The productive class buys $1000 manufactured goods from the manufacturing class. This now gives us the following holdings:

Productive Class	Proprietors	Manufacturing Class
$1000 food	$1000 food	$1000 food
$2000 raw materials	$1000 mfg'd goods	$1000 money
$1000 money		
$1000 mfg'd goods		

Step #5´: The manufacturing class buys $1000 raw materials from the productive class, which leads to:[75]

Productive Class	Proprietors	Manufacturing Class
$1000 food	$1000 food	$1000 food
$1000 raw materials	$1000 mfg'd goods	$1000 raw materials
$2000 money		
$1000 mfg'd goods		

Step #6´: Production and consumption take place. A surplus output is generated by the productive class, and by assumption #3´ the proprietors receive $2000 in rent claims. The situation now is:

Productive Class	Proprietors	Manufacturing Class
$2000 money	($2000 in rent claims)	$2000 mfg'd goods
$3000 food		
$2000 raw materials		

We have therefore returned to the position of original holdings.

Having set forth Tsuru's reconstruction of the *Tableau* in tabular form enables us to discern several problems and ambiguities.

First, the productive class possesses $1000 in raw materials whose

---

[75] This is the tabular equivalent of Tsuru's diagram #2, "On Reproduction Schemes", Appendix A, in Paul Sweezy, *The Theory of Capitalist Development*, p. 367.

role in production and exchange is not clear. The fact that these raw materials do not circulate, always remaining within the possession of the productive class, makes it seem as if Tsuru intends them to be an input into agricultural sector production.[76] But if this is so, then Step #6´, when production takes place, the productive sector, contra Quesnay, does not double its advances. Advances to productive sector workers would be $1000 each of manufactured goods, food, and raw materials, for a total of $3000. The output of the agricultural sector, however, is worth only $5000 ($2000 in raw materials and $3000 food) and $5000 is not twice $3000. On the other hand, it may be that the additional $1000 of raw materials is extraneous and does not play any substantive role in Tsuru's reproduction schema. Without explicit input-output assumptions from Tsuru though, it is not possible to determine what he meant.

Second, as with the Meek reconstruction, Tsuru implicitly assumes that manufactured goods are not an input in the production of manufactured goods. Again, even if we were to suppose that the manufacturing class possessed tools and machinery, but that these remained in the background of Tsuru's reconstruction of the *Tableau*, a problem remains nonetheless. For such tools and machinery would be used up and have to be replaced in the course of production. As with the Meek model, no provision is made within the Tsuru reconstruction for the replacement of such capital goods.

Finally, while Tsuru makes no explicit population or consumption assumptions, there are implicit assumptions built into his reconstruction that run counter to the actual assumptions made by Quesnay. For instance, Quesnay assumes that the consumption of all classes will be divided equally between the consumption of food and the consumption of manufactured goods (This is Meek's assumption #8). But the manufacturing class in the Tsuru reconstruction consumes *no* manufactured goods. At Step #6´, the manufacturing class consumes $1000 food and no manufactured goods when it produces manufactured goods. Also, as we have already shown, from Quesnay's population and consumption assumptions (Meek assumptions #5, #6 and #7), it follows that the total consumption of food by the manufacturing class must be half the total consumption of food by the productive class. But on Tsuru's reconstruction, total consumption of food is the same for both classes. Thus, either the

---

[76] This possibility was suggested to me by Ray Majewski.

population assumption or consumption assumptions must be violated. That is, either the population of the productive class must equal the population of the manufacturing class or the per capita consumption of food by the productive class is only half the per capita consumption of food by the manufacturing class.

Again, we see an attempt at reconstructing Quesnay's *Tableau* that is marred by problems.

SECTION III

The tabular approach to the mysteries of the *Tableau* appears to have first suggested by Henri Woog. Woog begins his reconstruction of the *Tableau* with the attribution of various holdings to the respective classes of society. He then goes on to discuss the particulars of exchange among these classes. However, Woog failed to provide the simple and clear sequence of tables which are of incalculable aid in understanding and visualizing the production of exchange relations that are supposed to take place. Woog also does not divide the output of the agricultural sector into raw materials and food goods as do Meek and Tsuru. Rather, all productive sector output is subsumed under the heading "agricultural goods."

Woog's reconstruction of the *Tableau* begins with the following assumptions:

(1*) through (4*), and (8*)—*Class Assumptions* and the *Input-Output Assumptions* are the same as assumptions (1) through (4) and (8).

(5*) through (7*) *Population Assumption* and *Consumption Assumptions*—No explicit population or consumption assumptions are made. Implicit assumptions about the population and consumption can be gleaned from the processes of production and exchange that Woog presents. These are discussed in the critique of Woog's reconstruction below.

(9*) *Endowments Assumption*—Woog begins with the assumption that the three classes are in possession of the following holdings:

Productive Class	*Proprietors*	*Manufacturing Class*
$2000 money	($2000 in rent claims)	$1000 money
$4000 agric'l goods		

Now Woog postulates six steps of circulation and production

which eventually bring us back to this position.[77]

Step #1*: The productive class pays the $2000 in rent it owes to the proprietors, which results in:

Productive Class	Proprietors	Manufacturing Class
$4000 agric'l goods	$2000 money	$1000 money

Step #2*: The manufacturing class purchases $1000 agricultural goods from the productive class and immediately transforms them into $1000 manufactured goods. The situation now is:

Productive Class	Proprietors	Manufacturing Class
$3000 agric'l goods	$2000 money	$1000 mfg'd goods
$1000 money		

Step #3*: The proprietors purchase $1000 agricultural goods and $1000 manufactured goods. This leads to:

Productive Class	Proprietors	Manufacturing Class
$2000 agric'l goods	$1000 agric'l	$1000 money
$2000 money	goods	
	$1000 mfg'd goods	

Step #4*: The manufacturing class purchases another $1000 agricultural goods from the productive class and again immediately transforms them into $1000 manufactured goods. This results in:

Productive Class	Proprietors	Manufacturing Class
$1000 agric'l goods	$1000 agric'l	$1000 mfg'd goods
$3000 money	goods	
	$1000 mfg'd goods	

Step #5*: The manufacturing class sells $1000 manufactured goods to the productive class. Holdings are now:

---

[77] These steps are laid out in Woog, *The Tableau Économique of François Quesnay*, p. 55f. I begin at Woog's step (iv), steps (i) to (iii) being merely introductory. Step #1* is included in Woog's (iv). Step #2* is Woog's step (v). Step #3* is the end of (v) and (vi) for Woog. Finally, Woog's step (vii) is broken down into two steps, Step #4* and Step #5*.

Productive Class	*Proprietors*	*Manufacturing Class*
$1000 agric'l goods	$1000 agric'l	$1000 money
$2000 money	goods	
$1000 mfg'd goods	$1000 mfg'd goods	

Step #6*: Production and consumption take placed in the agricultural sector resulting in the production of $4000 agricultural goods. Consumption by the proprietors also occurs, and by assumption #3*, the proprietors again have $2000 in rent claims. Making these changes we find that holdings are the same as in Woog's endowment assumption, #9*:

Productive Class	*Proprietors*	*Manufacturing Class*
$2000 money	($2000 in rent claims)	$1000 money
$4000 agric'l goods		

There are several problems here which are worthy of note.

First, at Steps #2* and #4* the manufacturing class takes $1000 agricultural goods and produces $1000 manufactured goods. In both instances manufactured goods are used neither as a means of production nor as a means of consumption by workers in the manufacturing sector. This is a problem which we have encountered previously in the reconstruction of both Meek and Tsuru.

Second, foreign trade does not figure into Woog's reconstruction, although it is an essential part of the *Tableau*. As we saw in Chapter II, the role Quesnay assigns to foreign trade comes out of his explanation of the *Tableau* rather than from the zig-zags themselves. In the zig-zags neither imports nor exports appear. But in his accompanying explanation, Quesnay notes that half of the agricultural products which the manufacturing class purchases are spent on foreign commerce.[78] The situation is as follows. The manufacturing class sells all the goods it produces to the productive class and proprietors. But according to Quesnay the manufacturing class must consume equal amounts of food and manufactured goods. Since there are no manufactured goods available internally, these goods must be obtained by the manufacturing class externally—that is, through foreign trade.

One way to overcome both of the above objections would be to postulate that at Steps #2* and #4*, when the manufacturing class

---

[78] Meek, *Economics of Physiocracy*, p. 109f., 121, 130, and *passim*.

receives $1000 agricultural goods, it immediately exports $500 of these and imports $500 manufactured goods. These $500 imported manufactured goods could then serve as inputs in the production of manufactured goods.

Although such an amendment is not in Woog, it is consistent with his explanation of the *Tableau*. However, it does not solve all the problems with Woog's reconstruction. Most important, for Woog the supply of money in the economy is one-and-one-half times as great as the surplus generated every year. Woog justifies employing this assumption on the ground that this is the only means of getting the *Tableau* to work. "Indeed," Woog writes, "solely the consideration of this additional unit of circulating money renders possible the actual reproduction of 2 units of revenue and the entire regeneration of the productive funds pertaining to the agricultural sphere."[79] If true, this would be an important contribution. It would show Quesnay was wrong in his assumptions and that the *Tableau* did not work exactly as he expected. However, Woog has *not* demonstrated the impossibility of reproduction with a smaller sum of money. In fact, as Section V will demonstrate, reproduction can take place with a stock of money equal to the agricultural surplus.

Finally, two additional problems with Woog's reconstruction require mention. First, Woog has manufacturing class advances solely in the form of money, which Quesnay denied. And second, in Woog's reconstruction, consumption and production take place at different times in each producing sector. As with Tsuru's reconstruction, this introduces an asymmetry into the *Tableau* which doubtless would have been unacceptable to Quesnay.

SECTION IV

Eltis' reconstruction focuses solely on the version of the *Tableau* published in "Analysis." Quesnay's zig-zag diagrams are ignored and attention focused instead on the formula version of the *Tableau*. Figure #3-1 provides Eltis' solution to the circulation and production relations of the *Tableau*.[80]

---

[79] Woog, *The Tableau Économique of François Quesnay*, p. 83.

[80] This figure is adopted from Figure 6 in Eltis, "Francois Quesnay: A Reinterpretation 1.", p. 193. I have amended Eltis' diagram by eliminating interest goods and including a dotted line to the right of "expenditure of wages of the productive class." Also, money figures have been converted to dollars.

Several explanatory remarks are in order here.

Numbers above the solid horizontal line which runs the length of the figure contain information concerning production by both the productive and manufacturing classes. Below this line we are presented with the exchanges which take place following production. Since the proprietors spend their revenue immediately and then disappear from all further transactions, their column is used by Eltis to provide an explanation of the exchanges which occur. The lines going to and from these explanations inform us as to the amount of

FIGURE #3-1

ELTIS' RECONSTRUCTION OF THE *TABLEAU*

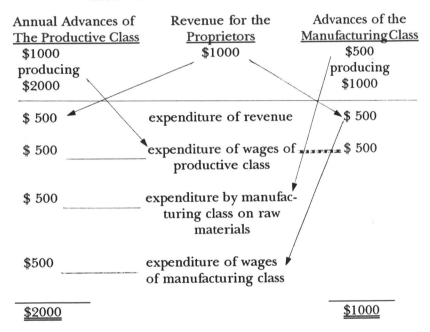

Annual Advances of The Productive Class	Revenue for the Proprietors	Advances of the Manufacturing Class
$1000 producing $2000	$1000	$500 producing $1000
$ 500	expenditure of revenue	$ 500
$ 500	expenditure of wages of productive class	$ 500
$ 500	expenditure by manufacturing class on raw materials	
$500	expenditure of wages of manufacturing class	
$2000		$1000

the transaction as well as the classes between which the exchange occurs. These are equivalent to the short statements describing the steps of exchange in previous sections. For example, the last line, "expenditure of wages of the manufacturing class," tells us that the manufacturing class purchases $500 of food from the productive class.

A factor not appearing in Figure #3-1, but nonetheless part of Eltis' reconstruction, is the foreign trade undertaken by the manufacturing class. This trade involves exporting $250 of food and importing $250 of manufactured goods.

The column totals, $2000 for the productive class and $1000 for the manufacturing class, represent money receipts for each class. Workers in the productive sector then produce $2000 of agricultural goods, which are sold for $2000 money. A portion of agricultural output is sold to other classes, and the remainder is sold internally to other productive sector workers. The line "expenditure of wages of the productive class" shows both internal and external sale of input. Here the productive class takes $1000 money, buying with it $500 agricultural goods (an internal sale) and $500 manufactured goods (an external sale). The latter exchange is represented by the dotted line, which I have added to Eltis' diagram.

Annual advances of the productive class according to Eltis are "the investment in raw materials, wages, etc., that must be made each year to produce a harvest."[81]   They are the inputs necessary for production in the agricultural sector—the manufactured goods and food needed to produce food and raw materials. Since inputs valued at $1000 result in the production of $2000 agricultural products, advances reproduce 100%, and a surplus of $1000 is created. This surplus is owed to the proprietors as rent. The figure that appears at the top of the proprietor's column represents the payment of this rent by the productive class. In the manufacturing sector, according to Eltis, "advances (principally raw materials which must be bought in advance) form half of industrial costs, so output is twice annual advances in both the 'productive' and the 'sterile' sectors."[82]

There are several interesting questions raised by these preliminaries and by Eltis' diagram of exchange between the classes.

First, it is odd that Eltis defines "advances" differently for the productive and the manufacturing classes. For the productive class advances include the food and manufactured goods necessary for production; but for the manufacturing class they are basically raw materials, and exclude the food and manufactured goods with comprise the other half of industrial costs. Excluding manufacturing sector wages from advances also makes it seem as if the manufacturing class has created surplus.

Furthermore, the second to the last exchange in Eltis' diagram—

[81] Ibid., p. 172.
[82] Ibid., p. 177.

"expenditure by the manufacturing class on raw materials"—is a purchase by the manufacturing class of $500 raw materials from the productive class. According to the lines connecting this explanation with monetary figures under column headings, the manufacturing class purchased these raw materials with its advances. But Eltis maintains that the manufacturing class already has raw materials as advances, and denies that the manufacturing class holds advances in the form of money. He states explicitly that the economy's stock of money is assumed to be $1000 and that the proprietors hold this money at the beginning of the circulation process.[83] This is represented by the $1000 in the proprietor's column of Figure #3-1. Moreover, Eltis criticizes Woog for suggesting that the manufacturing class holds advances in the form of money: "...this would make the money supply exceed total revenue (of the landed class), which would contradict Quesnay's several statements that it equals this."[84]   A similar problem arises with productive class wages. At the step "expenditure of wages of the productive class," the productive class purchases $500 agricultural goods and $500 manufactured goods with its advances.   These advances, however, are not money. Advances of the productive class are food and manufactured goods, and at the time these advances are supposed to be spent they have already been used to produce $2000 agricultural goods.

The above problems can be eliminated by making adjustments in Eltis' definition of "advances" and by making several changes in his diagram. What cannot be corrected is the lack of clarity inherent in reconstructions of the *Tableau* based upon the zig-zags or the formula. These models attempt to pack too much information into a space too small to accommodate it. Consequently, crucial aspects of the reproduction process are not represented. Even with Eltis' commentary on the nature of exchanges taking place it is never clear as we progress from step to step whether a particular class has the money to buy the goods it is supposed to purchase. In a general equilibrium model, where all exchanges take place simultaneously, this would not be a problem. But in a sequential model, where money functions as a means of exchange, money is absolutely necessary to purchase means of consumption and production. It facilitates the reproduction process. In contrast, a lack of money

---

[83] Ibid., p. 186.
[84] Ibid., p. 186 n2. Also see footnote 1.

hinders reproduction. Also unclear in both the zig-zag and formula variants of the *Tableau* are the inputs required in production, their proportions, and whether each class has the requisite inputs when production is supposed to occur. For a model of production by commodities these questions must be answered in order to demonstrate the viability of the model. Finally, the zig-zag and formula approaches suffer because they fail to include foreign trade as part of their diagrammatic solution. Instead, mention of trade is relegated to the status of a footnote, and its importance is easily missed. A single diagram attempting to show flows of goods, flows of money, production by means of commodities, and foreign commerce by means of a single line between numbers is bound to be both imprecise and confusing. This is one of the main reasons for the difficulty subsequent economists have had in understanding and interpreting the *Tableau*.

SECTION V

Thus we return to the tabular approach. This section contains a reconstruction of the *Tableau* in tabular form which is free of logical problems and which does not contradict any assumptions or assertions made by Quesnay. Because it is of tabular rather than of zig-zag form, all production and exchange relations are made clear and precise, and the reproduction process as depicted in the *Tableau* becomes readily comprehensible and sensible.

For this reconstruction we require the following assumptions:
$(1'')$ through $(7'')$—these assumptions are the same as assumptions (1) through (7).
$(8'')$ *Input-Output Assumptions.* We assume that \$X of inputs yields \$2X worth of output in the agricultural sector. In addition, we assume that in the productive sector, food and manufactured goods are the only inputs, and that they are to be used in equal amounts. In the manufacturing sector we assume that manufactured goods, in addition to raw materials and food, are needed as inputs in the production of manufactured goods. These are needed as means of consumption for the worker (clothing, shelter, etc.) and as means of production (tools and equipment). Following Quesnay, we suppose that \$X of food, \$X of manufactured goods, and \$2X of raw materials are needed to

produce $4X of manufactured goods.[85]

(9″) *Endowments Assumption.* The original holdings of each class following production by both the agricultural and productive sectors are as follows:

Productive Class	*Proprietors*	*Manufacturing Class*
$2000 money	($2000 in rent claims)	$2000 mfg'd goods
$3000 food		
$1000 raw materials		

It can now be postulated that the following six stages of exchange and production take place. Step #1″: The productive class pays $2000 to the proprietors as rent, as in our previous examples:

Productive Class	*Proprietors*	*Manufacturing Class*
$3000 food	$2000 money	$2000 mfg'd goods
$1000 raw materials		

Step #2″: The proprietors purchase $1000 food from the productive class and $1000 manufactured goods from the manufacturing class, again following previous reconstructions. The situation now becomes:

Productive Class	*Proprietors*	*Manufacturing Class*
$2000 food	$1000 food	$1000 mfg'd goods
$1000 raw materials	$1000 mfg'd goods	$1000 money
$1000 money		

Step #3″: The manufacturing class buys $1000 raw materials from the productive class, which results in:

Productive Class	*Proprietors*	*Manufacturing Class*
$2000 food	$1000 food	$1000 mfg'd goods
$2000 money	$1000 mfg'd goods	$1000 raw materials

Step #4″: The manufacturing class sells $1000 manufactured goods to the productive class, and then buys $1000 food with the money it receives. This step is the summation of all the zig-zags in the

---

[85] As Eltis, "Francois Quesnay: A Reinterpretation 1", p. 199, points out, "Quesnay states frequently through the various versions of the *Tableau* that the cost of the sterile sector are half wages and entrepreneurial incomes, and half raw materials."

original editions of the *Tableau*. Following these transactions we
have the following class holdings:

Productive Class	Proprietors	Manufacturing Class
$1000 food	$1000 food	$1000 food
$2000 money	$1000 mfg'd goods	$1000 raw materials
$1000 mfg'd goods		

Step #5″: The manufacturing class exports $500 food and imports
$500 foreign manufactured goods in accord with Quesnay's state-
ments on foreign trade. This leads to the position shown below:

Productive Class	Proprietors	Manufacturing Class
$1000 food	$1000 food	$ 500 food
$2000 money	$1000 mfg'd goods	$1000 raw materials
$1000 mfg'd goods		$ 500 mfg'd goods

Step #6″: Production and consumption take place, and by assumption #3″, the proprietors receive $2000 in rent claims. We have
now returned to our original situation:

Productive Class	Proprietors	Manufacturing Class
$2000 money	($2000 in rent claims)	$2000 mfg'd goods
$1000 raw materials		
$3000 food		

The above formula does not separate production and consumption in manufacturing as Meek did. Both take place in Step #6″,
where manufactured goods are produced by manufactured goods,
food, and raw materials. Nor does it make illicit assumptions about
money, advances, or production as the Woog and Eltis reconstructions required. Finally, the above reconstruction does not fall prey
to the ambiguities of Quesnay's zig-zags. Foreign trade, class
holdings, the exchange of money for commodities, and commodity
input requirements are all clearly shown in the series of tables above.

The foreign trade assumption that is employed here, that appears
in Quesnay, and that is contained as well as in most reconstructions
of the *Tableau*, warrants some further discussion. One potential
difficulty with this trade assumption is that it cannot hold for every
nation. If all countries had their population distributed in accord
with assumption #5″, every country would want to export food and
import manufactured goods. There would then be a dearth of

manufactured goods in the world. National economies would either cease to be viable—that is, they would not be able to reproduce themselves—or the domestic manufacturing sector would have to be developed and expanded in each nation. In the latter, case equilibrium would be reached when the population and output in manufacturing was 2/3 rather than half the population and output in agriculture. At this time the proprietors will comprise 3/13 of the population; the manufacturing class will increase to 4/13 of the population, and the productive class will be only 6/13 of the entire population.[86]   Then exchange can take place along the following lines, without any foreign trade, and with these original holdings:

Productive Class	*Proprietors*	*Manufacturing Class*
$2000 money	(\$2000 in rent claims)	$2666.67 mfg'd goods
$1333.33 raw materials		
$2666.67 food		

Step #1: The productive class pays $2000 to the proprietors as rent, which parallels our earlier examples:

Productive Class	*Proprietors*	*Manufacturing Class*
$1333.33 raw materials	$2000 money	$2666.67 mfg'd goods
$2666.67 food		

Step #2: The proprietors purchase $1000 food from the productive class and $1000 manufactured goods from the manufacturing class, again following previous reconstructions. At this point holdings are:

Productive Class	*Proprietors*	*Manufacturing Class*
$1333.33 raw materials	$1000 food	$1666.67 mfg'd goods
$1666.67 food	$1000 mfg'd goods	$1000 money
$1000 money		

Step #3: The productive class buys $1000 manufactured goods from the manufacturing class, and the manufacturing class buys $1000 raw materials from the productive class. This results in the following position:

---

[86] This change in the population distribution is necessary to keep per capita consumption in accord with assumption (6).

Productive Class	Proprietors	Manufacturing Class
$ 333.33 raw materials	$1000 food	$ 666.67 mfg'd goods
$1666.67 food	$1000 mfg'd goods	$1000 money
$1000 money		$1000 raw materials
$1000 mfg'd goods		

Step #4: The manufacturing class buys $333.33 raw materials and $666.67 food from the productive class. Now we have:

Productive Class	Proprietors	Manufacturing Class
$1000 food	$1000 food	$ 666.67 mfg'd goods
$2000 money	$1000 mfg'd goods	$1333.33 raw materials
$1000 mfg'd goods		$ 666.67 food

Step #5: Production and consumption takes place in accordance with Quesnay's input-output assumptions, and proprietors again receive $2000 in rent claims. This brings us back to the position of initial endowments:

Productive Class	Proprietors	Manufacturing Class
$2000 money	($2000 in rent claims)	$2666.67 mfg'd goods
$1333.33 raw materials		
$2666.67 food		

An alternative possibility, which allows for continued foreign trade, is to postulate the existence of a second country whose population distribution did not satisfy assumption #5″. In particular, such a country would have to have a population one-quarter the size of our original country, and distributed as follows: one-quarter of the population are proprietors, one-quarter comprise the productive sector, and the remaining one-half of the population are employed in the manufacturing or sterile sector. For such a country, exchange should occur along the following lines, assuming the original holdings given below:

Productive Class	Proprietors	Manufacturing Class
$ 250 money	($250 in rent claims)	$1000 mfg'd goods
$ 500 raw materials		

In this case, the proprietors' claims on the productive class is $1750 less than the amount in all our previous examples. $1500 of this decrease is the result of differences in the total population. The other $250 is the result of the decrease in agricultural laborers from one-half to one-quarter of the population. Both changes result in a drastic reduction of the surplus produced by the productive class. The proprietors may only claim this surplus as rent. If they claim more than this amount the economy will not be able to reproduce itself.

Also, it should be noted that in this example the productive class produces only raw materials. Since Quesnay did not allow raw materials to enter into foreign trade, the needs of the manufacturing class for raw materials must be met by the productive class. When the manufacturing class becomes a very large percentage of the population, as in this example, there is a great demand for raw materials (which comprise half of manufacturing sector inputs) and the productive class must produce just raw materials.

Given our initial holdings, exchange will take place along the following lines.

Step #1: The productive class pays $250 to the proprietors as rent, thus eliminating the proprietors' rent claims:

Productive Class	Proprietors	Manufacturing Class
$ 500 raw materials	$ 250 money	$1000 mfg'd goods

Step #2: The manufacturing class exports $500 manufactured goods and imports $500 food. This trade compliments that of Step #5″. The situation now stands:

Productive Class	Proprietors	Manufacturing Class
$ 500 raw materials	$ 250 money	$ 500 mfg'd goods
		$ 500 food

Step #3: The proprietors purchase $125 of manufactured goods and $125 of food, *both* from the manufacturing class,

Productive Class	Proprietors	Manufacturing Class
$ 500 raw materials	$ 125 mfg'd goods	$ 375 mfg'd goods
	$ 125 food	$ 375 food
		$ 250 money

Step #4: The manufacturing class buys $250 raw materials from the productive class. This exchange results in:

Productive Class	Proprietors	Manufacturing Class
$ 250 raw materials	$ 125 mfg'd goods	$ 375 mfg'd goods
$ 250 money	$ 125 food	$ 375 food
		$ 250 raw materials

Step #5: The productive class purchases $125 food and $125 manufactured goods from the manufacturing class. Now each class has the following holdings:

Productive Class	Proprietors	Manufacturing Class
$ 250 raw materials	$ 125 mfg'd goods	$ 250 mfg'd goods
$ 125 food	$ 125 food	$ 250 food
$ 125 mfg'd goods		$ 250 raw materials
		$ 250 money

Step #6: The manufacturing class purchases another $250 raw materials from the productive class, which results in:

Productive Class	Proprietors	Manufacturing Class
$ 125 food	$ 125 mfg'd goods	$ 250 mfg'd goods
$ 125 mfg'd goods	$ 125 food	$ 250 food
$ 250 money		$ 500 raw materials

Step #7: Production and consumption takes place, and the proprietors receive their rent claims. Holdings are thus:

Productive Class	Proprietors	Manufacturing Class
$ 250 money	($ 250 in rent claims)	$1000 mfg'd goods
$ 500 raw materials		

This returns us to the original position of holdings.

This last example shows how (with the right population assumptions) a country can generate an excess of manufactured goods but lack sufficient food, so that reproduction will require the export of manufactured goods and the import of food. The foreign trade assumption in our reconstruction of Quesnay's *Tableau* is then entirely reasonable. All that is required for the necessary foreign trade to occur is that there be another country whose population is one-quarter the size of the country depicted in Quesnay's static *Tableau*, and whose population distributed obversely.

Now that we have come to understand the workings of the static *Tableau*, we will relate the tabular reconstruction of the preceding section to the zig-zag versions of the *Tableau* and to Quesnay's formula. Let us again consider the zig-zag version of the *Tableau*, an example of which is reproduced below as Figure #3-2. Such a *Tableau* is provided at the end of the *Philosophie Rurale*, Volume I.

FIGURE #3-2

THE *TABLEAU* IN ZIG-ZAG FORM

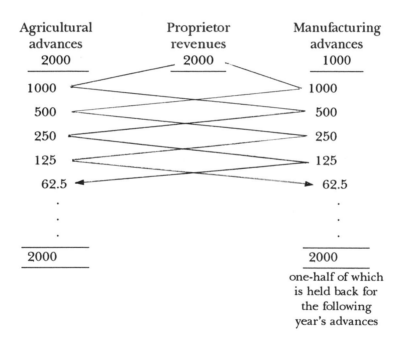

It is important to keep in mind that the zig-zags are only a small part of Quesnay's model and that a number of steps contained in the reconstruction of Section V do not appear in Quesnay's zig-zag diagram. The first line of Figure #3-2 represents proprietor receipts of rent due. This is equivalent to Step #1 of Section V. Note that the tabular reconstruction makes clear that the manufacturing sector holds $2000 manufactured goods, while the agricultural sector possesses $1000 worth of raw materials and $3000 of food. Figure #3-2 contains no such information. Class holdings must be inferred from the entire diagram and from Quesnay's explanatory notes.

The next line of Figure #3-2 represents the proprietor's spending their rent receipts. In accord with the assumptions of the static *Tableau*, half is spent on agricultural goods and half on manufactured goods. This is Step #2 of Section V.

According to the zig-zags, half the receipts of the sterile class are spent on manufactured good and half are spent on food. The same is true with respect to agricultural sector receipts. Hence the third line of Figure #3-2 shows the expenditure of $500 by the manufacturing sector on agricultural goods and $500 spent by the agricultural sector on maintained goods. These expenditures generate incomes for each producing sector, which again are spent half on food and half on manufactured goods. Thus line four shows the manufacturing sector spending $250 on agricultural goods and the agricultural sector spending $250 on manufactured goods. Successive lines represent the additional spending which takes place as a consequence of additional receipts by the two producing classes. Following proprietor spending, an arithmetic series develops. Each producing sector sells $500, then $250, then $125, then $62.50,... to the other producing sector. The entire progression results in the agricultural sector purchasing $1000 manufactured goods and the manufacturing sector buying $1000 food. This series of transactions, spatially a major portion of the *Tableau*, can be summarized into a single transaction. This was done by Quesnay in constructing the précis and the formula of the *Tableau* and by me in Step #4 of the reconstruction in Section V.

Steps #3, #5, and #6 have not been mentioned thus far. These steps involve the purchase of raw materials by the manufacturing sector, foreign trade, and production. None of them are shown in Figure #3-2, but they are important parts of Quesnay's reproduction model. In the course of exchange, the manufacturing sector sells $2000 worth of manufactured goods—$1000 to the proprietors and $1000 to the agricultural sector. This adds up to $2000, the column total for the manufacturing sector. The manufacturing sector, however, buys only $1000 worth of agricultural goods. They therefore have $1000 of money left over. This money cannot remain within the manufacturing sector since at the end of the production and exchange cycle, all money must be in the hands of the agricultural class according to Quesnay. Moreover, if each production cycle transfers money from the productive class to the manufacturing sector, the productive class will soon lack money to pay the proprietors. This will disrupt the circulation process, and cause the economy to decline. Step #3—the purchase of raw materials by the manufacturing sector—returns the $1000 to the agricultural class. This step is indicated in Figure #3-2 by Quesnay's note at the bottom of the sterile sector's column: of $2000 in manufacturing sector receipts, half is held back for next year's advances.

This remark, which appears at the bottom of all zig-zag *Tableaux*, has never been explained. Neither Quesnay nor his many interpreters explain why the manufacturing sector must hold back half its receipts as advances and why this is not true of the agricultural sector. Nor is it clear how money can be maintained by the manufacturing class and used as advances; they should have no money as advances. The solution to these puzzles is that Quesnay's note at the bottom of the sterile sector column is an indication that the sterile class takes half its money receipts and buys raw materials. The other half of the manufacturing sector's receipts cannot be held back in any sense because that money already has been used during the exchange period to buy food from the agricultural class. In contrast, the agricultural sector holds back no receipts because it engages in no purchases outside the zig-zags. One advantage of tabular representations over the zig-zags is that they make clear the necessity and importance of this transaction. Tabular reconstructions also demonstrate that the manufacturing sector has the money it needs to purchase raw materials.

Step #5 is the foreign trade step. This does not appear in the zig-zag diagram, but as we have seen in Chapter II, Quesnay's explanations all stress the importance of free trade, and his calculations were that foreign trade must be one-quarter of manufacturing sector output. This is the amount included in Step #5.

Finally, Step #6 of Section V also fails to appear in Figure #3-2. But the input-output assumptions contained in this step are required for reproduction to take place. They are also assumptions that are held by Quesnay. These are his famous dicta that the manufacturing sector is sterile and his contention that advances reproduce 100% in the productive sector. In manufacturing, the value of output must exactly equal the value of inputs employed. Since only manufactured goods are produced, $2000 worth of inputs result in the production of $2000 manufactured goods. In the productive sector, inputs double in value. $2000 worth of inputs become $4000 agricultural goods as a result of the bounty of nature. The difference—the net product produced in agriculture—must be paid to the proprietors in the form of rent payments. Consequently, in the table following Step #6, the proprietors are owed another $2000 by the productive class.

Quesnay soon came to realize that zig-zag presentations were useless for situations in which advances did not reproduce 100%. These problems led him to develop his formula and the précis of the *Tableau*. The formula first appeared in "The Analysis." This is the version reproduced as Figure #3-3.[87]

Two differences between the formula and the zig-zags should be readily apparent. The sequence of transactions between the two producing classes are now summarized in two transactions, and agricultural output has increased by 1 milliard. The latter change represents the incorporation of interest goods. Otherwise, the *Tableau* operates as before. Agriculture advances are $2000; proprietor rents are $2000; and manufacturing sector advances are $1000. Cultivators produce $5000 now instead of $4000, the additional $1000 representing interest goods. The manufacturing class takes its $1000 advances and its $1000 worth of raw materials and produces $2000 manufactured goods. Following rent payments to the proprietors, the proprietors spend half their income on agricultural goods and half on manufactured goods. This generates incomes and expenditures for the two producing classes, which up to now Quesnay showed with the zig-zags. This entire process is summarized by two transactions in the formula—the manufacturing sector's purchase of $1000 worth of agriculture goods and the agricultural sector's purchase of $1000 worth of manufactured goods.

Unfortunately, Quesnay draws the agricultural sector's purchase of manufactured goods from agricultural sector advances. As such, the formula creates the erroneous impression that manufactured goods are purchased with money held by the productive class as advances, despite the fact that the agricultural sector has no money as advances. In addition, towards the bottom of the column for the agricultural class, Quesnay shows this class spending all its advances within the agricultural sector. The 2 milliards in the expenditure column of the productive class is deemed by Quesnay "expenditure of agricultural advances." But if this is so, the agricultural class does

---

[87] Meek, *Economics of Physiocracy*, p. 158.

FIGURE #3-3
FORMULA OF THE *TABLEAU*
Total reproduction: Five milliards

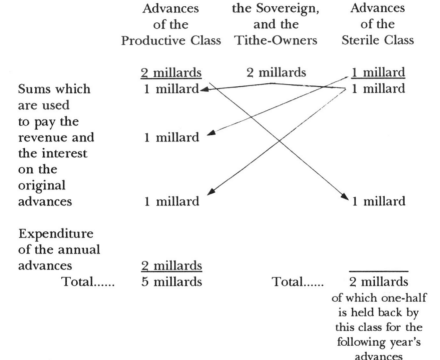

	Annual Advances of the Productive Class	Revenue for the Proprietors of the Land, the Sovereign, and the Tithe-Owners	Advances of the Sterile Class
	2 millards	2 millards	1 millard
Sums which are used to pay the revenue and the interest on the original advances	1 millard		1 millard
	1 millard		
	1 millard		1 millard
Expenditure of the annual advances	2 millards		
Total......	5 millards	Total......	2 millards

2 millards of which one-half is held back by this class for the following year's advances

not have an additional 1 milliard of advances that it can spend on manufactured goods. The solution to these puzzles is that the agricultural class receives money from the proprietors during the circulation process. It is this money that is used to buy manufactured goods.

A similar problem arises with respect to the purchase of food by themanufacturing sector. Quesnay has the manufacturing class use its advances to buy food. Again, the manufacturing class has no money advances. However, they do receive money from the sale of manufactured goods. It is the food that the manufacturing class purchases with this money that becomes manufacturing sector advances.

Figure #3-4 corrects the problems we have seen with the formula. Advances are no longer used by the producing sectors to purchase commodities, and the agricultural sector spends internally only the amount of its advances. The reproduction process depicted in Figures #3-4 is that which has been carefully described in this chapter.

FIGURE #3-4

CORRECTED FORMULA OF THE *TABLEAU*

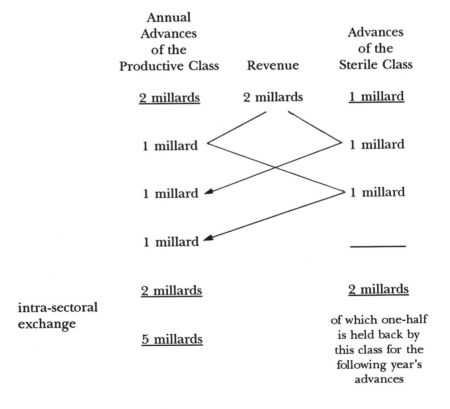

Annual Advances of the Productive Class	Revenue	Advances of the Sterile Class
2 millards	2 millards	1 millard
1 millard		1 millard
1 millard		1 millard
1 millard		

| intra-sectoral exchange | 2 millards | | 2 millards |
| | 5 millards | | of which one-half is held back by this class for the following year's advances |

CHAPTER IV
A RECONSTRUCTION OF TIIE DYNAMIC *TABLEAU*

Despite the fact that most commentators have devoted their attention to the static *Tableau*, simple reproduction was not Quesnay's primary concern. Rather, his real goal was to explain the processes of economic growth and decline. Quesnay sought to understand the reasons for the demise of the French economy because he wanted to set forth economic policies to remedy this situation.

The analysis of these problems requires a dynamic *Tableau*, one capable of showing growth and decline. In Chapter II we looked at several instances of the dynamic *Tableau*. But as with the static model, Quesnay failed to provide an adequate explanation of these *Tableaux*. Nor did he provide an explanation or mechanism detailing the process by which an economy grows or declines. We are again faced with a model of seeming obscurity.

This chapter will attempt to explain the workings of the dynamic *Tableau*. As in the preceding chapter, before reaching this stage previous reconstructions will be examined.

There have been three main attempts to explain the dynamic *Tableau*. Meek and Woog each tackle the dynamic *Tableau* following their reconstructions of the static *Tableau*, and Robert Eagly provides a third reconstruction in *The Structure of Classical Economic Theory*.[88] These three works will be examined in Sections I, II, and III respectively. The reconstructions will be explained and subject to critical analysis. As in Chapter III, objections will be raised on several accounts—for attributing to Quesnay what he expressly denies, for failing to explain particular mechanisms, and for logical or mathematical errors. Finally, Section IV provides what I believe is a satisfactory explanation of the dynamics of Quesnay's *Tableau*. It contains no illegitimate assumptions and sets forth

---

[88] See Robert V. Eagly, *The Structure of Classical Economic Theory* (New York: Oxford University Press, 1974), Chapter 2, "The Quesnaysian Revolution and the Birth of Classical Theory," pp. 10-33. This chapter first appeared in a slightly different form as "A Physiocratic Model of Dynamic Equilibrium," *Journal of Political Economy*, 77 (1969), 66-84.

methodically the steps and mechanisms by which an economy grows and declines. It also remains faithful to the assumptions and assertions of Quesnay. But first, we return to Meek.

SECTION I

Meek's reconstruction of the dynamic *Tableau* involves little more than reproducing the *Tableaux* set forth by Quesnay in *Philosophie Rurale* and *L'Ami des Hommes*. His depiction of economic decline as a result of all classes spending 3/5 of their receipts on manufactured goods and 2/5 on food is reproduced below.[89]

FIGURE #4-1

THE DYNAMIC *TABLEAU* IN DECLINE

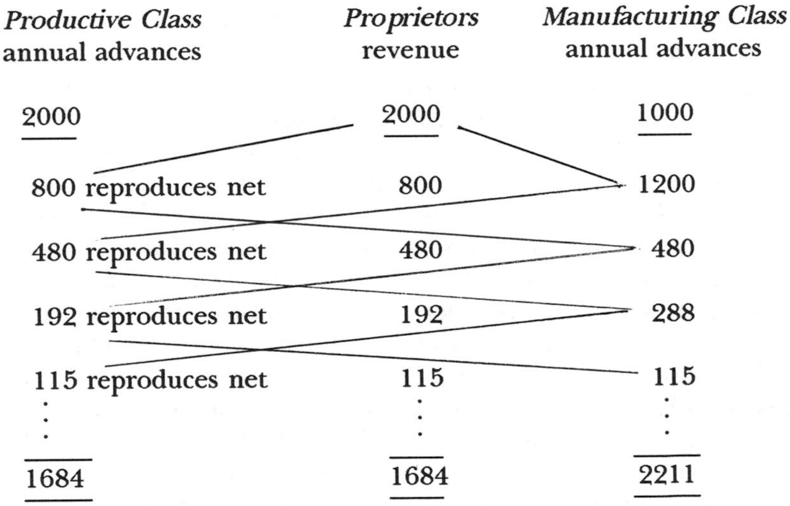

Productive Class annual advances	Proprietors revenue	Manufacturing Class annual advances
2000	2000	1000
800 reproduces net	800	1200
480 reproduces net	480	480
192 reproduces net	192	288
115 reproduces net	115	115
.	.	.
.	.	.
1684	1684	2211

We begin in static equilibrium with a base of $2000. Proprietors then spend 3/5 of their revenue, or $1200, on manufactured goods, and only 2/5, or $800, on the food of the productive sector. Both producing classes likewise spend 3/5 of their money

---

[89] This diagram is taken from Meek, *Economics of Physiocracy*, p. 288.

receipts on manufactured goods and 2/5 on food. Thus the sterile class buys $1200 x 2/5 = $480 food and the productive class buys $800 x 3/5 = $480 manufactured goods. This new spending generates additional income for the two producing classes, which again is spent 3/5 on manufactured goods and 2/5 on food. The manufacturing class buys $192 food and the productive class buys $288 manufactured goods. Again spending generates additional income, which in turn generates spending in the assumed proportions. Total expenditure on agricultural goods as a result of the zig-zags will be $1684. This is equal to proprietor expenditures of $800 plus the sum of all manufacturing sector purchases of food. This latter figure will be equal to $884. Total expenditure on manufactured goods as a result of the zig-zags will be $2211. This is the sum of proprietor expenditures on manufactured goods plus agricultural sector expenditures on manufactured goods. Proprietors spend $1200 on manufactured goods. Agricultural sector purchases of manufactured goods will be $1011.[90] Total output following the change in spending propensities will be $5579 (=$1684 + $1684 + $2211). There has been a decline from the previous year's output of $6000 ($4000 agricultural goods + $2000 manufacturing goods). Proprietor rents also fall from $2000 to $1684 because the argicultural surplus has declined.

    In succeeding years the decline in proprietor incomes, again multiplied by the new spending propensities, will result in a further decline in output and incomes. Output in the manufacturing sector will drop below its original $2000 in the very next production period. Meek does not provide us with a diagram demonstrating this result; however, a zig-zag diagram for the next period is not difficult to construct.

    As Meek points out, the changes in output in the preceding period give rise to a change in proprietor revenues in the next period. The agricultural surplus has declined to $1684, so proprietor incomes will fall to this figure. Of the $3368 agricultural goods produced by the agricultural sector, half constitute the agricultural surplus, which generates financial obligations on the part of the agricultural sector to the proprietors. The other half will be used as annual advances by the agricultural sector in the next period. Similarly, the manufacturing sector uses half its output as annual

---

advances (while the other half, as we saw in Chapter III, goes to purchase raw materials from the productive sector). Beginning with these advances and revenues, and continuing to assume that all classes spend 3/5 of their receipts on manufactured goods and 2/5 on food, we can represent exchange and production in the next period by the following table:[91]

FIGURE #4-2

TABLEAU WHEN SPENDING PROPENSITIES OF THE PRODUCING
CLASSES ARE THE REVERSE OF PROPRIETOR PROPENSITIES

Productive Class annual advances	*Proprietors* revenue	*Manufacturing Class* annual advances
1684	1684	1105.5
674 reproduces net	674	1010
404 reproduces net	404	404
162 reproduces net	162	242
97 reproduces net	97	97
.	.	.
.	.	.
.	.	.
1418	1418	1861

Total output is now down to $4697 and manufacturing sector output is below $2000. In the third production period, proprietor revenues decline to $1418. This again reduces spending on both agricultural and manufactured goods. Manufacturing sector revenue in the third period becomes $1567 and receipts of the productive class become $1194. In general, when all classes spending 3/5 on manufactured goods and 2/5 on food, agricultural sector output and manufacturing sector output decrease approximately 16% per

---

[91] Receipts for both producing classes can be derived by generalizing the results of Appendix #1. This is done in Appendix #2. In the second period, R = $1684, making agricultural sector receipts $1418 and manufacturing sector receipts $1861.

annum.   Eventually output will approach 0 for both producing sectors as smaller revenues reduce the demand for and output of agricultural goods which, in turn, further reduces proprietor revenues.   Thus Meek concludes: "looking at the process as it continues over several years, everyone will lose; nothing can arrest the process of decline other things being equal, except an increase in the propensity to consume agricultural produce."[92]

On the other hand, if all classes spend more than half their incomes on agricultural goods, things work in reverse. The economy grows rather than declines. Starting from static equilibrium with a base of $2000 and reversing spending propensities, the analysis of the preceding pages is reversed. In the next period agricultural incomes and output rise to $2211, while manufactured output is $1684. This increases proprietor's revenues to $2211.   In succeeding periods there is then further spending and further increases in output and proprietor incomes.

The   problems   with   these   diagrams,   and   with   Meek's accompanying analysis, are similar to the problems we noted with the zig-zags in Chapter III.   There we saw that the *Tableau* was only a small part of Quesnay's model.   Moreover, the zig-zags fail to demonstrate a number of necessary conditions for reproduction. They do not make clear whether the agricultural and manufacturing classes have the requisite inputs for production to take place. They also fail to take into account money flows. Thus we cannot show that each class has a sufficient quantity of money to buy the goods it needs to produce commodities. Finally, the zig-zags do not show several transactions which nonetheless must take place during the circulation process. In particular, foreign trade and the purchase of raw materials by the manufacturing class are not shown in the *Tableau*'s zig-zags.

Several new problems also arise. First, the *Tableau* is a model of the production of commodities by means of commodities.[93]   As such, the basic determinant of each producing sector's output is the quantity of inputs used in production. These inputs, like the output produced, are commodities. Let us consider now what happens when every class spends 3/5 of its income on manufactured goods and 2/5 on agricultural goods. The productive sector,

---

[92] Meek, *Economics of Physiocracy*, p. 288.

[93] This phrase is, of course, due to Sraffa. See the references and quotations in footnote #145 of Chapter 5.

as we have seen, sells $800 food to the proprietors and $884 to the manufacturing sector. Total food sold is worth $1684, as the column total for the productive class in Figure #4-1 shows. Yet, before the change in spending propensities the agricultural sector produced $4000 agricultural goods. When spending propensities change, $1684 rather than $2000 agricultural goods are sold, and $2316 rather than $2000 remain. This *should increase* agricultural output in the next period, since agricultural sector workers have *more* agricultural inputs with which to produce agricultural goods. In addition, the productive sector has increased its purchase of manufactured goods. Thus it has more of both inputs needed to produce agricultural goods. It seems then that the agricultural sector should be growing. It is not clear how or why it produces less.

A similar problem arises with respect to the manufacturing sector. Before the change in spending propensities artisans produced $2000 of manufactured goods. Yet Figure #4-1 shows that a change in spending proportions results in $2211 manufactured goods sold to the productive class and to the proprietors. Meek does not explain the origin of the additional $221 of manufactured goods. Nor does he clarify the mechanism whereby the artisans create a surplus. Manufacturing sector workers start the production process depicted in Figure #4-1 with only $2000 of inputs, and then produce $2211 of manufactured outputs. This seeming surplus violates Quesnay's firm conviction that the manufacturing sector was always sterile. Finally, it is not clear how the manufacturing sector can increase production if they do not generate a surplus. To produce $2211 of manufactured goods, the manufacturing sector must use more agricultural and manufactured goods. But the manufacturing sector purchases less food according to the new consumption assumption. In addition, more manufactured goods have been purchased by the proprietors and productive class. This leaves fewer manufactured goods to serve as inputs in the next year's production of manufactured goods. These points can be illustrated by attempting to transform Figure #4-1 to tabular format. We proceed as in Chapter III. The only difference will be consumption assumption (7) which is now

> (7′) All classes spend 2/5 of their income on agricultural goods and 3/5 of their income on manufactured goods.

Following production and the payment of rent to the proprietors, each class holds the following:

Productive Class	Proprietors	Manufacturing Class
$3000 food	$2000 money	$2000 mfg'd goods
$1000 raw materials		

Step #1: The proprietors spend their rental incomes. In line with our new consumption assumption, (7´), they buy $800 food and $1200 manufactured goods. Holdings become:

Productive Class	Proprietors	Manufacturing Class
$2200 food	$ 800 food	$1200 money
$1000 raw materials	$1200 mfg'd goods	$ 800 mfg'd goods
$ 800 money		

Step #2: We now begin to represent the zig-zags, starting with the manufacturing class purchasing $884 food. This results in:

Productive Class	Proprietors	Manufacturing Class
$1316 food	$ 800 food	$ 316 money
$1000 raw materials	$1200 mfg'd goods	$ 884 food
$1684 money		$ 800 mfg'd goods

Step #3: The other portion of the zig-zags requires that the agricultural class purchase $1011 manufactured goods. At this time the manufacturing sector possesses only $800 manufactured goods. Additional manufactured goods must therefore be obtained. The obvious means of obtaining more manufactured goods is through import. We have already seen that foreign trade is an integral part of Quesnay's model. So let us conjecture that at this point $211 food is exported by the manufacturing sector, and $211 of manufactured goods is imported. Class holdings become:

Productive Class	Proprietors	Manufacturing Class
$1316 food	$ 800 food	$ 316 money
$1000 raw materials	$1200 mfg'd goods	$ 673 food
$1684 money		$1011 mfg'd goods

Step #4: We can now complete the zig-zag transactions. The agricultural class purchases $1011 manufactured goods. This gives us:

Productive Class	Proprietors	Manufacturing Class
$1316 food	$ 800 food	$1427 money
$1000 raw materials	$1200 mfg'd goods	$ 673 food

$ 673 money
$1011 mfg'd goods

Step #5: The manufacturing sector purchases $1000 raw materials, resulting in:

Productive Class	Proprietors	Manufacturing Class
$1316 food	$ 800 food	$ 427 money
$1673 money	$1200 mfg'd goods	$ 673 food
$1011 mfg'd goods		$1000 raw materials

At this stage in the static model the manufacturing sector engages in foreign trade. Then we have production and consumption; and the economy should be ready to begin the next year's reproduction cycle. But consider what would happen here if production took place following foreign trade. The manufacturing sector could produce at most $1673 of manufactured goods since it has only $1673 worth of inputs. Making matters worse, it has the wrong proportions of inputs. The manufacturing sector has excess raw materials and food, but no manufactured inputs. Despite this shortfall of inputs, according to the zig-zag diagram manufacturing sector output should increase to $2211. On the other hand, the productive sector possesses inputs valued at $2327. Assuming inputs reproduce 100%, agricultural output in the next period will be $4654. This constitutes *an increase* in agricultural output rather than the $316 reduction we find in Figure #4-1. Even requiring that equal amounts of food and manufactured goods be used—thereby letting $205 food go to waste—the economy still produces $4044 agricultural goods. So this cannot solve our problem. Rather, it demonstrates the problem discussed above. An increase in demand for the commodities of a sector reduces the inputs available to that sector, which should reduce production; less demand for a sector's output makes available more inputs, and hence makes possible greater output in the future.

A second problem with Meek's explanation of the *Tableau* is his assumption that all three classes will change their spending propensities in the same manner. Assumption (7´) had the two producing classes, in addition to the proprietors, purchase more manufactured goods than before. No reason is given, however, to suppose that the producing classes will follow the proprietors' example. Good reasons exist why they may not. The producing classes consume agricultural goods at or near subsistence level. The proprietors though, by assumption (6) from Chapter III, consume twice as much food per capita as members of the producing classes. They are thus able to reduce their consumption of food and increase their consumption of manufactured goods. For the producing classes, on the other hand, it will be detrimental to reduce their consumption of food below the requirements of subsistence. Thus it is unlikely that they will follow the lead of the proprietors and consume more manufactured goods and less food.

It is more likely that any change in the spending propensity of the producing classes will be the *reverse* of the proprietors' change. When the proprietors consume more manufactured goods, fewer manufactured goods remain for the producing sectors to buy. These sectors must then buy relatively more food and relatively less manufactured goods. Also, it will be in the interest of those in the producing sectors to maintain the current level of production. In general, when proprietor spending favors manufactured goods it is possible to maintain the level of output if and only if productive and sterile class spending propensities are the reverse of the proprietors' spending propensities. When the proprietors spend 3/5 of their income on manufactured goods, only if the two producing classes spend 3/5 of their incomes on food the economy will reproduce itself. The zig-zag diagram of Figure #4-3 demonstrates this result:[94]

---

[94] Because the proprietors and producing classes spend differently, the sequence, S_n, of manufacturing sector purchases of food differs too. Now,

$S_n = \$2000(3/5)^2 + \$2000(3/5)(2/5)^2 + \$2000(3/5)^3(2/5)$
$\quad + \$2000(3/5)^3(2/5)^3 + \$2000(3/5)^4(2/5)^2 + ...$

and

$S_n(3/5)(2/5) = \$2000 (3/5)^3(2/5) + \$2000(3/5)^3(2/5)^3 +$
$\qquad \$2000(3/5)^4(2/5)^2 + \$2000(3/5)^3(2/5)^4 + ...$

So,

$S_n = \dfrac{\$2000(3/5)^2 + \$2000(3/5)(2/5)^2}{1-(3/5)(2/5)} = 1200$

The proprietors spend 2/5 ($2000) = $800 on food, making total food demand $1200 + $800 = $2000.

The sequence representing agricultural sector purchases of manufactured goods is the same as S_n, except that the fractions 3/5 and 2/5 are reversed.

$S_n = \dfrac{\$2000(2/5)^2 + \$2000(2/5)(3/5)^2}{1-(3/5)(2/5)} = 800$

Total demand for manufactured goods is thus $800 + $1200 (the proprietors demand for manufactured goods) = $2000.

FIGURE #4-3

TABLEAU WHEN SPENDING PROPENSITIES OF THE PRODUCING CLASSES
ARE THE REVERSE OF PROPRIETOR PROPENSITIES

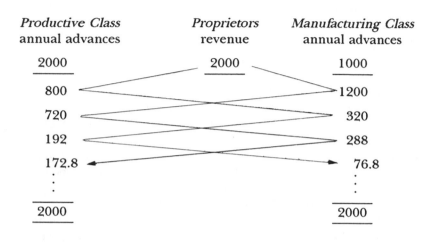

Productive Class annual advances	*Proprietors* revenue	*Manufacturing Class* annual advances
2000	2000	1000
800		1200
720		320
192		288
172.8		76.8
⋮		⋮
2000		2000

Meekian tables can also be used to demonstrate that the economy
continues to reproduce without decline. Following rent payments by
the productive class to the proprietors, holdings are:

Productive Class	*Proprietors*	*Manufacturing Class*
$3000 food	$2000 money	$2000 mfg'd goods
$1000 raw materials		

In conformity with consumption assumption (7´) the proprietors
purchase $800 food and $1200 manufactured goods. This gives us:

Productive Class	*Proprietors*	*Manufacturing Class*
$2200 food	$ 800 food	$ 800 mfg'd goods
$1000 raw materials	$1200 mfg'd goods	$1200 money
$ 800 money		

Next we have the zig-zag step. Our new assumption is that the
producing classes each spend 3/5 of their incomes on agricultural
goods and 2/5 on manufactured goods. Figure #4-3 shows, and

footnote 94 proves, that the productive class must buy $800 of manufactured goods and the manufacturing class must buy $1200 of food. Class holdings are now:

Productive Class	Proprietors	Manufacturing Class
$1000 food	$ 800 food	$ 800 money
$1000 raw materials	$1200 mfg'd goods	$1200 food
$1200 money		
$ 800 mfg'd goods		

The manufacturing sector exports $700 food and imports $500 manufactured goods and $200 raw materials, resulting in:

Productive Class	Proprietors	Manufacturing Class
$1000 food	$ 800 food	$ 500 food
$1000 raw materials	$1200 mfg'd goods	$ 500 mfg'd goods
$1200 money		$ 200 raw materials
$ 800 mfg'd goods		$ 800 money

The manufacturing sector purchases $800 raw materials from the agricultural sector. Now we get:

Productive Class	Proprietors	Manufacturing Class
$1000 food	$ 800 food	$ 500 food
$ 200 raw materials	$1200 mfg'd goods	$ 500 mfg'd goods
$2000 money		$1000 raw materials
$ 800 mfg'd goods		

At this stage the manufacturing sector has the inputs it needs to produce $2000 manufactured goods. To produce $4000 agricultural goods the productive sector needs an additional $200 manufactured goods. It also has $200 extra raw materials. One way to remedy this problem would be for the productive sector to sell or loan $200 raw materials to the manufacturing sector, who then export it. In return, manufactured goods are imported, which are resold or repaid to the agricultural class. Another possibility is a change in input-output assumptions. A portion of agricultural inputs go to feed agricultural workers. If these workers decide to consume more food and less manufactured goods, input requirements will rise for food and fall for agricultural goods in the agricultural sector.[95] Agricultural sector workers then can produce $200 fewer raw materials and $200 more food, and consume the additional food. In either case, the agricultural sector will have the inputs necessary for next year's production. Production and consumption can then take place, returning us to our initial holdings.

Meek's presentation of the dynamic *Tableau* fails then because he provides us only with zig-zags. There is no accompanying explanation of the workings of the dynamic *Tableau*. There is no justification of the assumption that all classes will simultaneously spend more on manufactured goods, and no recognition that the producing classes cannot reduce their consumption of food below subsistence requirements. Finally, and most importantly, Meek has not seen the input-output problem of the dynamic *Tableau*.

SECTION II

In this section we will look at Woog's attempt to explain the dynamic *Tableau*.[96] Woog follows Meek in presenting the dynamic *Tableau* in zig-zag form. However, Woog's analysis contains a significant advance because Woog offers some mechanisms that attempt to explain how the dynamic *Tableau* operates.

The reason that spending propensities of all classes are the same, according to Woog, stems from the preeminent position of the proprietor in society. Proprietors set the standards of taste and are the models for appropriate behavior. When they consume more luxury, manufactured goods and reduce expenditures on agricultural goods, "this reversed attitude towards the consumption of the necessities of life in favor of secondary commodities pertaining to the manufacturing sphere influences retrospectively the morals and habits of the entire community."[97] As moral leaders and trend

---

[95] The same is true, of course, for the manufacturing sector. Any change in input-output assumptions within the manufacturing sector can be handled at Step #3. Increased food requirements and reduced manufacturing requirements will reduce exports of food imports of manufactured goods.

[96] Henri Woog, *The Tableau Économique of François Quesnay* (Switzerland: A. Francke A.G. Verlag Bern, 1950), pp. 82-98.

[97] Woog, *The Tableau Économique of François Quesnay*, p. 84. Cf. Sir James Steuart, *An Inquiry into the Principles of Political Economy*, Vols. I-IV of *The Works of Sir James Steuart* (New York: Augustus M. Kelley, 1967), Book I, esp. Chapters 1, 3, and 5. Steuart has the statesman set standards of taste for society. The state, of

setters, any pattern of consumption adopted by the proprietors will win approval and be adopted by the producing classes. Thus an increase in the propensity of the proprietors to consume manufactured goods results in identical behavior by the other classes.

Given that all classes will spend their incomes in the same manner, we can now demonstrate economic growth and decline. Woog here follows Meek by providing a zig-zag diagram showing the reduction in output and proprietor rents as society consumes more manufactured goods. A *Tableau* with a base of 1050 livres is used. Woog assumes that all classes spend 7/12 of their incomes on manufactured goods and 5/12 on food.[98] Otherwise Woog's diagram is identical to Meek's diagram, which is reproduced as Figure #4-1.

Woog though moves beyond Meek analytically by providing a mechanism to explain the reduction in agricultural output when the demand for agricultural goods declines. This mechanism is a change in relative prices. When demand for agricultural goods falls, there is a "a sinking of prices in agricultural products. The pendant to this development is represented by a rise in the prices of manufactured goods caused by intensified effective demand for products of the sterile class."[99] Woog argues that this interpretation is supported by Quesnay's repeated maxims that a high price for agricultural goods is necessary for a healthy, growing economy.[100]

---

course, is included in the *Tableau* as part of the proprietary class.

[98] Woog, *The Tableau Économique of François Quesnay*, p. 85.

[99] Ibid., p. 86.

[100] Remarks by Quesnay to this effect appear at several places. The first reference to the importance of high agricultural prices is in the Encyclopedia article "Corn": "not only is the proper price favorable to the progress of agriculture, but it is also in the proper price itself that the wealth which agriculture procures consists" (Meek, *Economics of Physiocracy*, p. 84). Again, "it is very harmful to allow a people to get used to buying corn at too low a price. As a result they become less hard-working; they spend little on the bread they eat and become lazy and presumptuous..." (Meek, *Economics of Physiocracy*, p. 86). Each edition of the *Tableau* also contains a warning about the deleterious effects of a low price for food. Remark 13 which accompanies the first edition of the *Tableau* contains the assumption "That people do not believe that cheapness of produce is profitable to the lower classes; for a low price of produce causes a fall in their wages, reduces their well-being, makes less work or remunerative occupations for them, and reduces the nation's revenue" (Meek, *Economics of Physiocracy*, p. 113.). An identical statement can be found as maxim 13 of "The Royal Economic Maxims of M. de Sully." This is appended to the second and third editions of the *Tableau*. See Meek, *The Economics of Physiocracy*, p. 122 and Marguerita

In order to make Woog's proposal clear, let us transform his zig-zags into Meekian tables. We start from a situation of static equilibrium. Now, however, we must account for quantities as well as prices. To keep things simple, let us assume that 1 unit of manufactured goods has a price of $1 and 1 unit of food is sold for $1. We also assume raw materials cost $1 per unit. Our new assumption will be a price assumption to the effect that an X% change in demand results in a Y% change in price in the same direction. For simplicity it will be assumed that X=Y. So when the demand for food changes by 20% its price will fall by 20%, to $.80. The per unit price of manufactured goods will increase to $1.20, since the demand for manufactured goods increases by 20%. The price of raw materials will be assumed to remain constant. Following rent payments by the productive class each class has in its possession the following:[101]

Productive Class	Proprietors	Manufacturing Class
$3000 food	$2000 money	$2000 mfg'd goods
(3000 units)		(2000 units)
$1000 raw materials		
(1000 units)		

The proprietors spend their incomes—2/5 on food and 3/5 on manufactured goods. This increases the price of manufactured goods and reduces the price of food purchases by the proprietors. Each class now has:

Productive Class	Proprietors	Manufacturing Class
$1600 food	$1200 mfd'd goods	$1200 mfg'd goods
(2000 units)	(1000 units)	(1000 units)
$1000 raw materials	$ 800 food	$1200 money
(1000 units)	(1000 units)	(1000 units)
$ 800 money		

Via the zig-zags, the manufacturing class buys $884 food and the productive class purchases $1011 manufactured goods. This transaction gives us:

Kuczynski and Ronald L. Meek, *Quesnay's Tableau Économique* (New York: Augustus M. Kelley, 1972), p. 10.

[101] In the reconstruction below quantities are given in parentheses following the values of each sort of holding.

Productive Class	Proprietors	Manufacturing Class
$ 716 food	$1200 mfd'd goods	$ 189 mfg'd goods
(895 units)	(1000 units)	(157.5 units)
$1000 raw materials	$ 800 food	$1327 money
(1000 units)	(1000 units)	$ 884 food
$ 673 money		(1105 units)
$1011 mfg'd goods		
(842.5 units)		

The artisans buy raw materials from the agricultural class, resulting in:

Productive Class	Proprietors	Manufacturing Class
$ 716 food	$1200 mfg'd goods	$ 189 mfg'd goods
(895 units)	(1000 units)	(157.5 units)
$1673 money	$ 800 food	$ 327 money
$1011 mfg'd goods	(1000 units)	$ 884 food
(842.5 units)		(1105 units)
		$1000 raw materials
		(1000 units)

The manufacturing class now engages in foreign trade. To maximize production the manufacturing sector should export $469.4 food (586.75 units) and import $36.5 raw materials (36.5 units) and $432.9 manufactured goods (360.75 units). It is assumed that international prices are the same as domestic prices in the intersectoral market. Following these exchanges, we have:

Productive Class	Proprietors	Manufacturing Class
$ 716 food	$1200 mfd'd goods	$ 621.9 mfg'd goods
(895 units)	(1000 units)	(518.25 units)
$1673 money	$ 800 food	$ 327 money
$1011 mfg'd goods	(1000 units)	$ 414.6 food
(842.5 units)		(518.25 units)
		$1036.5 raw materials
		(1036.5 units)

We are now ready for production and consumption to take place. Obviously this must follow our input-output assumption *in quantity terms*, for it is quantities of food and manufactured goods that are necessary to produce quantities of output. In the manufacturing sector, 518.25 units each of food and manufactured goods, plus 1036.5 units of raw materials, will be combined to produce 2073

units of manufactured goods. The value of these goods will be
$2487.60 in the intersectoral market. Though this is greater than
the value we obtained using Figure #4-1, it is an increase in the
value of manufactured goods produced, and it does show how a price
increase for manufactured goods can result in additional output of
manufactured goods.

In the productive sector I will relax the requirement that
equal quantities of food and manufactured goods need to be
employed and assume that 895 units of food and 842.5 units of
manufactured goods are used to produce 1737.5 units of agricultural
goods. This is done for the purpose of demonstrating that agricultural output falls even when we make the most contrary assumptions
possible. Assuming that equal proportions of food and manufactured
inputs are necessary will reduce agricultural output even further, as
several units of food will go to waste rather than to producing
agricultural goods. Approximately 1303 units of the 1737.5 units of
agricultural goods produced will be food, and approximately 434.5
units will be raw materials. This follows previous cases in which 3/4
of the productive sector's output was food and 1/4 was raw materials.
The value of the food produced will be $1042.4., and the value of
raw materials $434.5. In agriculture, then, price reductions lead to
reductions in output.

In this example, real income is transferred from agriculture
to manufacturing as a consequence of changes in price. Real
consumption by the proprietors is unchanged—they still consume
1000 units apiece of food and manufactured goods. However, the
increased price of manufactured goods reduces the quantity of
manufactured goods which the agricultural sector can buy. This
leaves more manufactured goods to served as inputs in manufacturing and also reduces manufactured inputs available to agriculture.
Contrariwise, the fall in food prices increases the quantity of food
which the manufacturing sector buys and so increases the available
inputs in manufacturing. This is, of course, balanced by a reduction
in food inputs available to the agricultural sector. Therefore, there
is an increase in real manufactured output and a reduction in real
agricultural output.

This example makes clear that price changes can be analyzed
using the *Tableau* and can provide an explanation for the workings
of the dynamic *Tableau*. It is not clear, however, that Quesnay had
such price changes in mind as a mechanism of the dynamic *Tableau*.
Quesnay seems to regard demand as one factor determining the

price of agricultural goods, but is wedded to a cost of production theory with respect to manufactured goods. In the "Dialogue on the Work of Artisans" he writes: "It is the expense of the labor which determines the price of the artisans' goods, and the competition of the latter sets limits to the expense of their labor."[102] Demand is unimportant here. The supply of labor determines the cost of employing labor and this cost determines the price of manufactured goods.

Likewise, Quesnay's repeated assertions that the manufacturing sector was sterile and generated no surplus belies the possibility that changes in the price of manufactured goods could be the mechanism that explains the workings of the dynamic *Tableau*. For when prices of manufactured goods increase, a profit is generated in the manufacturing sector. As we have just seen, output produced at a cost of $2000 gets sold for $2400 when demand increases the price of manufactured goods. This profit is the price equivalent of a surplus in the manufacturing sector.

Woog's suggestion of price changes for both agricultural and manufactured goods cannot therefore be what Quesnay intended. Let us consider now what happens if just agricultural prices change. We assume, as before, that reduced demand lowers the price of food by 20%.

At the outset holdings and their values are:

Productive Class	Proprietors	Manufacturing Class
$3000 food	$2000 money	$2000 mfg'd goods
(3000 units)		(2000 units)
$1000 raw materials		
(1000 units)		

Proprietor spending—3/5 on manufactured goods and 2/5 on food—yields:

Productive Class	Proprietors	Manufacturing Class
$1600 food	$1200 mfg'd goods	$ 800 mfg'd goods
(2000 units)	(1200 units)	(800 units)
$ 800 money	$ 800 food	$1200 money
$1000 raw materials	(1000 units)	
(1000 units)		

---

[102] Meek, *Economics of Physiocracy*, p. 288. Similar sentiments are expressed in the *Encyclopedia* articles "Corn" and "Men."

As part of the zig-zags the manufacturing class buys $884 of food. This results in:

Productive Class	Proprietors	Manufacturing Class
$ 716 food	$1200 mfg'd goods	$ 800 mfg'd goods
(895 units)	(1200 units)	(800 units)
$1000 raw materials	$ 800 food	$ 316 money
(1000 units)	(1000 units)	$ 884 food
$1684 money		(1105 units)

For the other half of the zig-zags, the agricultural sector buys $1011 manufactured goods. The manufacturing sector has only $800 manufactured goods at this time however. One source of additional manufactured goods is foreign countries. So we will let the manufacturing sector export $211 food (263.75 units) and import $211 manufactured goods (211 units). Foreign trade gives the manufacturing sector sufficient manufactured goods to sell to the agricultural sector.

Productive Class	Proprietors	Manufacturing Class
$ 716 food	$1200 mfg'd goods	$1011 mfg'd goods
(895 units)	(1200 units)	(1011 units)
$1000 raw materials	$ 800 food	$ 316 money
(1000 units)	(1000 units)	$ 673 food
$1684 money		(841.25 units)

This sale of manufactured goods completes the zig-zags and makes class holdings:

Productive Class	Proprietors	Manufacturing Class
$ 716 food	$1200 mfg'd goods	$1327 money
(895 units)	(1200 units)	$ 673 food
$1000 raw materials	$ 800 food	(841.25 units)
(1000 units)	(1000 units)	
$ 673 money		
$1011 mfg'd goods		
(1011 units)		

The manufacturing class now buys raw materials, giving us:

Productive Class	Proprietors	Manufacturing Class
$ 716 food	$1200 mfg'd goods	$ 327 money
(895 units)	(1200 units)	$ 673 food

$1673 money	$ 800 food	(841.25 units)
$1011 mfg'd goods	(1000 units)	$1000 raw materials
(1011 units)		(1000 units)

To maximize production the manufacturing sector should export $320.75 of food (401 units) and $109.5 of raw materials (109.5 units), while importing $440.25 of manufactured goods (440.25 units). As a result of this foreign trade class holding are now:

Productive Class	*Proprietors*	*Manufacturing Class*
$ 716 food	$1200 mfg'd goods	$ 327 money
(895 units)	(1200 units)	$ 352.25 food
$1673 money	$ 800 food	(440.25 units)
$1011 mfg'd goods	(1000 units)	$ 880.5 raw materials
(1011 units)		(880.5 units)
		$ 440.25 mfg'd goods
		(440.25 units)

At this point production and consumption should take place, with manufacturing output increasing and agricultural output declining. Note however that the problems from Section I have returned. The manufacturing sector produces only 1761 units or $1761 of manufactured good because it has fewer inputs. Even if the manufacturing sector were to buy additional inputs with its $327 money it would still produce just barely more than $2000 manufactured goods. It will not be able to produce $2211 manufactured goods.

But there are even more serious problems here. The manufacturing sector takes inputs valued at $1673 ($352.25 food, $880.5 raw materials, and $440.25 manufactured goods) and produces manufactured goods valued at $1761 (1761 units of manufactured goods). This profit is the price equivalent of a surplus for the manufacturing sector. But if the manufacturing sector produces a surplus this cannot be a description of Quesnay's dynamic *Tableau*. Price changes then cannot be the mechanism we are looking for to understand the dynamic *Tableau*.

Two final points are worth noting concerning this price mechanism advanced by Woog. First, the sort of economy Quesnay depicts in the *Tableau*—one with free foreign trade—should have relatively stable prices. Quesnay makes this point quite clearly. In the *Encyclopedia* article "Men" he writes: "Prices... are never subject to big variations in a kingdom with an import and trade with other nations which is mutual, unobstructed, and perfectly free: because prices in such a kingdom are equal to the common prices which are current in the other countries."[103]   Price changes then do not seem to be the mechanism Quesnay had in mind. Second, all the *Tableaux* drawn by Quesnay, including those demonstrating economic growth and decline, are in price terms. The proprietors in Figure #4-1 begin with $2000 and end with $1684. In Figure #4-2 proprietors' revenue declines again. Productive sector receipts likewise fall. These reductions in money receipts are intended by Quesnay to represent economic decline. But this will be true if and only if prices are constant. If receipts of the agricultural class fall, but the price of agricultural goods declines by a greater percentage, the agricultural sector will have more inputs available and the economy will grow in real terms. The fact that Quesnay did not concern himself with analyzing what was happening to the economy in real terms, but contented himself with showing growth and decline in nominal terms, shows that price changes were not intended to be the mechanism by which the dynamic *Tableau* operates. We must look elsewhere then. In the next section we look at Eagly's solution.

SECTION III

Eagly's explanation of the dynamic *Tableau*[104] is neither terms of zig-zags nor a series of tables. Algebraic equations are used instead.   For both the demand and supply side of each sector, equations are derived showing the factors upon which demand or supply depend. Demand depends upon proprietor revenues and the spending propensities of each class, while supply depends upon the advances made in a particular sector.   Equilibrium exists when supply equals demand in all sectors. To account for the growth and decline of an economy, changes in capital or advances are introduced into the equations.

A set of definitions is necessary at the outset.   These definitions will then be used to derived a series of equations representing the relations of the *Tableau*. Following Eagly we let:

$$R \quad = \quad \text{rental income of proprietors}$$
$$Q_a \quad = \quad \text{quantity of agricultural commodities}$$

---

[103] Ibid., p. 94; also see, p. 171.
[104] Eagly, *The Structure of Classical Economic Theory*, pp. 10-33.

Q_m	=	quantity of manufactured commodities
C	=	annual advances of the agricultural sector
C*	=	annual advances of the manufacturing sector
K	=	original advances of the agricultural sector
K*	=	original advances of the manufacturing sector
d	=	the rate of depreciation
A	=	gross output of the agricultural sector
M	=	gross output of the manufacturing sector
a	=	the propensity of the productive class to purchase manufactured goods
r	=	the propensity of the proprietors to purchase agricultural goods
l-r	=	the propensity of the proprietors to purchase manufactured goods
b	=	the propensity of the manufacturing sector to purchase agricultural goods
π	=	the percentage rate of profit on total capital employed in the productive sector
ß	=	the percentage rate of profit on total capital employed in the manufacturing sector
α	=	the ratio of output to annual advances in the agricultural sector. On Quesnay's assumption, α = A/C = 2.
ρ	=	the ratio of output to annual advances in the manufacturing sector. On Quesnay's assumptions, ρ = M/C* = 1.
q	=	the ratio of original to annual advances in the manufacturing sector. q = K*/C*.

Consider first the manufacturing sector. The demand for manufactured goods comes from 2 sources—proprietors and agricultural workers. Proprietors' income in the current period is R, and they spend l-r of their income on manufactured goods. So (l-r)R is spent on manufactured goods by the proprietors. Agricultural workers spend a fraction, a, of their income on manufactured goods. Their income is a series $rR + b(l-r)R + abrR + ab^2(l-r)R + a^2b^2rR + ... + a^nb^{n-1}rR + a^nb^n(l-r)R$, which sums to $[rR + b(l-r)R]/(1-ab)$. Agricultural workers thus spend a $[rR + b(1-rR)]/(1-ab)$ on manufactured goods. Total demand for manufactured goods, Q^D_M, is thus

$$(1) \quad Q^D_M = (l-r)R + \frac{arR}{1-ab} + \frac{ab(l-r)R}{1-ab} = \left[\frac{l-r+ar}{1-ab}\right]R$$

It should be noted that Eagly assumes there is no demand for manufactured goods from the manufacturing sector because his reconstruction is in terms of supply and demand "on the intersectoral market.[105]   This market, of course, is the market represented by Quesnay's zig-zags. *Intra*sectoral transactions are not shown in the *Tableau*.

Intersectoral demand for agricultural goods comes from 3 sources— proprietors, manufacturing sector incomes, and manufacturing sector demand for raw materials.   Proprietors spend the fraction, r, of their income on agricultural goods, so demand rR of agricultural goods. Via the zig-zags, the manufacturing class receives a stream of income equal to $(l-r)R + arR + ab(l-r)R + a^2brR + a^2b^2(l-r)R + ... + a^nb^{n-1}rR + a^nb^n(l-r)R$. This sums to $[(l-r)R + arR]/1-ab$. A fraction, b, of this is spent on agricultural goods, so $b[(l-r)R + arR]/1-ab$ is the second component of the intersectoral demand for agricultural goods.   Finally, the manufacturing sector must purchase raw materials from the agricultural class.   The demand for raw materials according to Eagly will be equal to the quantity of money held by the manufacturing class after the completion of all zig-zag transactions.   Otherwise the economy's money will not be returned to the productive sector during the exchange process. This, in turn, will hamper reproduction in succeeding years. We have already derived figures for manufacturing sector receipts and manufacturing sector food purchases. These figures are $R[l-r+ar]/(l-ab)$ and $R[b(l-r)+ar]/(l-ab)$ respectively. Their difference, $R[(l-b)(l-r+ar)]/(l-ab)$, is the third source of demand for agricultural goods. Total intersectoral demand for agricultural goods, Q_A^D, is the sum of its three components:

$$(2) \quad Q_A^D = rR + \frac{R(b(l-r+ar))}{l-ab} + \frac{R((l-b)(l-r-ar))}{l-ab} = \frac{R(l+ar(l-b))}{l-ab}$$

For the static *Tableau*, where $a = b = r = .5$, and $R = 2000$, $Q_M^D = \$2000$, and $Q_A^D = \$3000$.   This agrees with the figures of Chapter III.

On the supply side, M is the total supply of manufactured goods. Supply on the intersectoral market will be M less any demand for manufactured goods by the manufacturing class. Capitalists in

---

[105] Ibid., p. 26.

the manufacturing sector will want some manufactured goods to replace depreciated original advances. Original advances depreciate by dK^*, the rate of depreciation times manufacturing sector original advances. Manufacturing sector capitalists will also want manufactured goods to increase their original advances. Net additions to fixed capital in the manufacturing sector is given by βK^*, the rate of profit in the manufacturing sector times the fixed capital employed. Manufacturing sector demand for manufactured goods is thus $(\beta + d)K^*$,[106] and the intersectoral supply of manufactured goods is:

$$(3) \quad Q^S_M = M - (\beta + d)K^*$$

Multiplying and dividing by C^* gives us

$$(4) \quad Q^S_M = C^* [M/C^* - (\beta + d) (K^*/C^*)] = C^* [(\rho - q (\beta+d)]$$

Gross agricultural output is A. The agricultural sector uses part of A to replenish annual advances and increase original advances. Annual advances in the productive sector are C, which is the amount that must be replaced. The rate of profit is π, so πC is the agricultural output used to increase advances. Total <u>intra</u>sector demand for agricultural goods is $(1 + \pi) C$, and $A - (1+\pi)C$ is supplied on the *inter*sectoral market. Since $\alpha = A/C$, $A = \alpha C$, and the intersectoral supply of agricultural goods can be expressed as:

$$(5) \quad Q^S_A = C (\alpha - (1 + \pi))$$

The static *Tableau* is based on the assumption that $\rho = 1$ and $\alpha = 2$. These are Quesnay's assumptions that the manufacturing sector is sterile and productive sector output is twice the value of its inputs. Moreover, in the static case, $\beta = d = \pi = 0$, and $C = C^* = \$2000$. This makes $Q^S_M = \$2000$ and the intersectoral market for manufactured goods is in equilibrium. However, $Q^S_A = \$2000$ rather than $\$3000$. There is no equilibrium in the intersectoral agricultural market, and the above equations fail to demonstrate static equilibrium in the *Tableau*.

Disequilibrium in the agricultural sector stems from a logical

---

[106] Intrasectoral demand for manufactured goods does not include demand to replace working capital because the manufacturing class obtains manufactured goods for this purpose through foreign trade.

slip involving the intersectoral supply of agricultural goods. Eagly assumes that all annual advances received by the productive sector come from agricultural output, A. Productive sector advances, though, are used to buy both manufactured goods and food. Only a fraction of advances, a, will be used internally to buy food. We must deduct aC from A to derive the intrasectoral supply of agricultural goods, in addition to πC. This makes the intersectoral supply of agricultural goods:

(6) $Q_A^S = C (\alpha - a + \pi)$

When C = \$2000, $\alpha = 2$, a = .5, and $\pi = 0$, $Q_A^S = \$3000$. This equilibrates the intersectoral market for agricultural goods.

Having established static equilibrium using Eagly's equations let us move on to the dynamic situation. We again consider the effects of all classes spending 3/5 of their income on manufactured goods and 2/5 of their income on agricultural goods. This makes r = .4, a = .6, and b = .4. We know that given these values the intersectoral supply and demand of manufactured goods should increase to \$2211. Intersectoral supply and demand for agricultural goods will be \$1684 plus manufacturing sector demand for raw materials. Eagly's equations, however, give us very different results.

(1*) $Q_M^D = R \left[\dfrac{1-r+ar}{1-ab} \right] = 2000 \left[\dfrac{1-.4+.24}{1-.24} \right] = 2210.5$

(2*) $Q_A^D = R \left[\dfrac{1+ar(1-b)}{1-ab} \right] = 2000 \left[\dfrac{1+.24(.6)}{1-.24} \right] = 3010.5$

(3*) $Q_M^S = C* (\varrho - q(d + \beta)) = 2000 (1-0) = 2000$

(4*) $Q_A^S = C (\alpha - a \pi q) = 2000 (2 - .6 - 0) = 2800$

Neither intersectoral market is in equilibrium. In both cases demand is greater than supply. The only correct figure is for Q_M^D in equation (1*). As equation (3*) shows, the intersectoral supply of manufactured goods remains at the static level of $2000. This is really the same problem that we have encountered throughout this chapter. Given a fixed value of inputs from the previous period, how can demand for more manufactured goods increase the value of output without generating a surplus? Eagly's equations have not solved this problem.

Intersectoral supply of agricultural goods decreases to $2800. This is almost equal to intersectoral demand for food based upon the zig-zags ($1684) plus manufacturing sector demand for raw materials ($1105.75 = 1/2 the value of manufactured goods produced). However, inexplicably, intersectoral demand for agricultural goods has risen (equation 2*). Since this figure depends just upon spending propensities and proprietor rents, something has clearly gone wrong with Eagly's equations. The problem it seems is Eagly's assumption concerning the demand for raw materials. Eagly maintained this would be equal to the quantity of money held by the manufacturing sector following the zig-zags. Though this is true in the static case, it does not hold in the dynamic case. In the static case, the reason all money must be returned to the productive class is that the money supply is equal to proprietor rents. If the manufacturing class holds some money, the productive class will be unable to pay the entire rent it owes the proprietors. Lower proprietor incomes will then cause reduced demand for both agricultural and manufactured goods, and the economy will decline. In the dynamic case of economic decline, the agricultural surplus and rent payments will both fall. The productive class therefore does not need to hold the entire money supply. A look back at the tabular reconstruction on pages 79 and 80 will help illustrate this point. After the completion of the zig-zags, following Step #4, the manufacturing class has $1427 of money. It needs only $1105.75 of raw materials for next period's production. In addition, the agricultural sector will need only $1684 of money in the next period, since its surplus will be only $1684 because of the reduced demand for agricultural goods. If we add $1105.75 to the money the productive sector holds after Step #4, it will have $1678.75, which will nearly suffice for next year's rent. The manufacturing class will have all the raw materials it needs plus $321.5 money left over. There is no reason to assume that this left over money will also go to purchase agricultural goods. The manufacturing sector and the proprietors have all the agricultural goods they need. By making the excess money held by the manufacturing class part of the intersectoral demand for agricultural goods, Eagly has created excess demand for agricultural goods.

Finally, let us consider again the insufficient supply of manufactured goods. Given equation (3*), there are only four ways that Q_M^S can increase to $2211: (1) ρ can increase, (2) q can decrease, (3) d can decrease, or (4) β can decrease. None of these possibilities, though, makes any sense. Since $\rho = M/C^*$, it must be equal to 1. If it increases above 1, the manufacturing sector produces a surplus, which Quesnay would not allow. There is likewise no reason for q, the ratio of original to annual advances in the manufacturing sector, to decrease. Moreover, we began from the static case where d = β = 0. So even if q falls, unless d or β also fall Q_M^S will remain constant. But there is no reason to assume either will fall when the demand for manufactured goods increases. If anything, increased demand for manufactured goods will increase the rate of profit (β) in the manufacturing sector and increase the rate of depreciation (d) as capital is used more intensively. Again we find ourselves at a loss to explain how the supply of manufactured goods can increase. Again we lack a mechanism explaining the workings of the dynamic *Tableau*. And again we are left with the impression that the *Tableau* rests on some sort of mathematical legerdemain.

SECTION IV

The major difficulty with reconstructions of the dynamic *Tableau* can be stated succinctly. Quesnay maintained that when the demand for a commodity increases, the output of that commodity increases. His model, however, is one of the production of commodities by commodities. Inputs are necessary for production. Increased demand reduces available inputs to a sector. How then can output increase? To make matters worse, Quesnay assumed that in the manufacturing sector the value of inputs was equal to the value of the output produced. A change in the value or price of the commodities produced cannot explain how the value of manufacturing sector output increases.

What we need is an explanation of how output can increase when demand increases. This mechanism must explain how a sector can produce more when it sells more and has fewer inputs available for production. It must also explain how the value of output in the manufacturing sector can increase when demand increases. Finally, it must be a mechanism that Quesnay recognizes.

Such a mechanism is the one which closed the static version of the *Tableau* in Chapter III. It is a population mechanism whereby changes in spending propensities result in changes in the composition of the population.

This mechanism was clearly recognized by Quesnay and incorporated into his economic system. We saw in Chapter II that Quesnay noted the affect of demand on population. In "Corn," he writes: "Manufacturers and artisans gather together in a country only in proportion to the current revenue of the nation, that is in proportion to the existence of proprietors or merchants who are able to buy their goods at prices which are about as high as those for which they could sell them elsewhere."[107]   Again, "Population increases much more through revenue and expenditure than it does through the propagation of the nation itself. Revenue increases expenditure, and expenditure attracts men who seek gain;...".[108]

Quesnay here envisions the influx and outflow of foreign laborers as the cause of the changes in the composition of the domestic population. But there is no reason why the composition of the domestic population may not itself change. More demand for manufactured goods and less demand for agricultural goods thus entails a shift in the domestic population from the agricultural to the manufacturing sector. This movement is equivalent to an inflow of artisans from abroad and an exodus of agricultural workers to foreign nations.

In "Men," where Quesnay was most concerned with population it is again revenue, or demand generated by the spending of revenue, that determines the number of inhabitants in a nation. "The population of a state increases in the proportion that the nation's revenue increases, because the revenue procures well-being and gains by which men are maintained and attracted."[109]   In this passage Quesnay's concern is with the entire population. However, the principle proffered should apply as well to the distribution of the population among the sectors of the economy. When demand for the goods produced by one sector increases, employment opportunities in that sector increase, and men are attracted to that sector. The

---

[107] Meek, *Economics of Physiocracy*, p. 75.

[108] Ibid., p. 84.

[109] Ibid., p. 88.

sector experiencing a reduction in demand will need fewer workers. Some of the workers who cannot find employment there will migrate abroad, or to the sector experiencing an increase in demand.

This population mechanism is also incorporated into the *Tableau*. All editions of the *Tableau* contain calculations of a sector's population for given revenues. In the first edition, the explanatory notes at the left of the productive class column calculate the population that can subsist, given proprietor revenues. "The proprietor, who spends the revenue of 400 livres, draws his subsistence from it. The 200 livres distributed to each expenditure class can support one man in each; thus 400 livres of revenue enable three heads of families to subsist. On this basis 400 millions of revenue can enable three million families to subsist, estimated at three persons above the age of infancy per family."[110] Similar calculations are carried out in the "Economic Maxims of M. de Sully."[111] In *L'Ami des Hommes* the mechanism is developed in greater detail. There Quesnay makes it clear that "population goes where there is employment" and that "increased expenditure attracts men to the kingdom."[112]

It is not sufficient, though, if just the population changes. For population changes do not explain how manufacturing output can increase when demand increases. Two things must occur in addition. The transfer of inputs or means of subsistence must accompany the migration of workers, and there must be changes in agricultural sector productivity. Quesnay recognized both these consequences of a change in the composition of the population. "If [farmers] are harassed into abandoning the countryside and withdrawing to the towns, they take their fathers' wealth which used to be employed in cultivation."[113] Reduced capital in the agricultural sector will then reduce agricultural productivity. "The advances of the farmers are sufficient to enable the expenses of cultivation to reproduce at least 100 percent; for if the advances are not sufficient,

---

[110] Ibid., p. 110.

[111] For calculations in the second edition v. Meek, *Economics of Physiocracy*, p. 120; for population calculations in the third edition v. Kuczynski and Meek, *Quesnay's Tableau Économique*, p. 1f.

[112] Victor de Riquetti, Marquis de Mirabeau and Francois Quesnay, *L'Ami des Hommes* (Amsterdam: Chez Les Libraires Associes, 1764), Vol. V, pp. 88 and 107 respectively. The translations are my own.

[113] Meek, *Economics of Physiocracy*, p. 112.

the expenses of cultivation are higher and produce little net revenue."[114]

From Figure #4-1 it is clear that manufacturing output must increase to $2211. Only if working capital or annual advances accompany the worker to the manufacturing sector is it possible for the manufacturing sector to begin with inputs of $2000 and end the circulation and production process with $2211 manufactured goods, while creating no surplus. Capitalist farmers, those who possess annual advances in the agricultural sector, must move then to the manufacturing sector in addition to workers. Capitalist farmers become capitalist merchants, manufacturers and traders in the manufacturing sector. Their wage fund becomes new advances in the manufacturing sector. More workers can be hired now in the manufacturing sector, and there are more inputs available. In addition, the reduction in capital in the productive sector will reduce productivity in that sector, as "grande" agriculture becomes "petite."

For manufactured output to increase to $2211, $221 worth of inputs must be transferred from the agricultural to the manufacturing sector. If agricultural advances continue to reproduce 100%, agricultural output would decline by $442. But production should decline by $632 according to Quesnay's zig-zags. The explanation for this additional decline can only by a change in agricultural sector productivity. When capital is removed from agriculture, "petite" agriculture replaces "grande" agriculture, and average productivity on the land declines.[115] Of course, manufacturing productivity never changes. The manufacturing sector is always sterile.

It should be pointed out here that this population mechanism differs significantly from that of Smith, Malthus, and Ricardo. For these thinkers, population growth depended upon the difference between real and subsistence wages. Quesnay's population mechanism is really a capital allocation mechanism. Advances, which are the capital in Quesnay's model, move from sector to sector as a consequence of changes in demand for the output of the respective sectors. This supports Eagly's position that "Quesnaysian economics

---

[114] Ibid., p. 112.

[115] See Meek, *Economics of Physiocracy*, pp. 131, 81; Francois Quesnay, *Francois Quesnay et la Physiocratie* (Paris: Institut National d'Études Demographiques, 1958), pp. 450-452; and Joseph J. Spengler, "Mercantilist and Physiocratic Growth Theory," Bert Hoselitz et. al. *Theories of Economic Growth* (Glencoe: Free Press, 1960), p. 60f.

is classical economics "[116] because it embraced the capital allocation problem which Eagly believes is the central problem of classical economics.

The two mechanisms described above, in conjunction with a sequence of Meekian tables, will now be used to explain the workings of the dynamic *Tableau*. First we look at the case of economic growth. We begin, as usual, with the following holdings:

Productive Class	Proprietors	Manufacturing Class
$3000 food	$2000 money	$2000 mfg'd goods
$1000 raw materials		

The proprietors spend 2/5 of their incomes on manufactured goods and 3/5 on food. When other classes do likewise, this will result in the production of $4422 agricultural goods and $1684 manufactured goods in the next period. We will see how circulation, exchange, population changes, and productivity changes in agriculture generate this result. Proprietor spending gives us the following:

Productive Class	Proprietors	Manufacturing Class
$1800 food	$ 800 mfg'd goods	$1200 mfg'd goods
$1000 raw materials	$1200 food	$ 800 money
$1200 money		

The manufacturing sector receives $884 from the agricultural class, which purchases manufactured goods. This represents one portion of the *Tableau*'s zig-zags, and results in:

Productive Class	Proprietors	Manufacturing Class
$1800 food	$ 800 mfg'd goods	$ 316 mfg'd goods
$1000 raw materials	$1200 food	$1684 money
$ 316 money		
$ 884 mfg'd goods		

The agricultural sector receives $1010 from the manufacturing sector. This represents the purchase of food by the manufacturing sector through the zig-zags. Following all zig-zag transactions, holdings are:

---

[116] Eagly, *The Structure of Classical Economic Theory*, p. 10. I am indebted to Ray Majewski for this point.

Productive Class	Proprietors	Manufacturing Class
$ 790 food	$ 800 mfg'd goods	$ 316 mfg'd goods
$1000 raw materials	$1200 food	$ 674 money
$1326 money		$1010 food
$ 884 mfg'd goods		

Now we consider the effect of these expenditures on the population. The new spending propensities force manufacturing sector workers to find employment in agriculture. Capitalists in the manufacturing sector become capitalist farmers. Since the manufacturing sector will produce $1684 manufactured goods and no surplus, it is easy to calculate the change in inputs accompanying the population shift. Output decreases by $316, so inputs must do likewise. I will assume that $158 manufactured goods and $158 food become part of the advances of the agricultural sector. Original advances are also transferred from manufacturing to agriculture. This will affect agricultural productivity when production takes place. The change in population and inputs gives us:

Productive Class	Proprietors	Manufacturing Class
$ 948 food	$ 800 mfg'd goods	$ 158 mfg'd goods
$1000 raw materials	$1200 food	$ 674 money
$1326 money		$ 852 food
$1042 mfg'd goods		

The manufacturing class sells $211 food abroad. There is no return purchase. This transaction constitutes a trade surplus, which is necessary in order to obtain additional money for the economy. Since the agricultural surplus will increase to $2211 next period, an additional $211 money will be needed by the agricultural sector to pay the proprietors. The only way to obtain money is to incur a trade surplus, and the only class that engages in foreign trade is the manufacturing class. Holdings are now:

Productive Class	Proprietors	Manufacturing Class
$ 948 food	$ 800 mfg'd goods	$ 158 mfg'd goods
$1000 raw materials	$1200 food	$ 885 money
$1326 money		$ 641 food
$1042 mfg'd goods		

The manufacturing class purchases raw materials. It has only $885 to spend on raw materials, so only $885 of raw materials can be purchased. This transaction transfers the additional money to the productive class as can be seen below:

Productive Class	Proprietors	Manufacturing Class
$ 948 food	$ 800 mfg'd goods	$ 158 mfg'd goods
$ 115 raw materials	$1200 food	$ 641 food
$2211 money		$ 885 raw materials
$1042 mfg'd goods		

The manufacturing sector exports $43 raw materials, $220 food, and imports $263 manufactured goods, resulting in:

Productive Class	Proprietors	Manufacturing Class
$ 948 food	$ 800 mfg'd goods	$ 421 food
$ 115 raw materials	$1200 food	$ 842 raw materials
$2211 money		$ 421 mfg'd goods
$1042 mfg'd goods		

The manufacturing class can now produce $1684 of manufactured goods in accordance with Quesnay's input-output assumptions. The productive class must transform $115 raw materials into an equivalent value of food and manufactured goods. This can be done through foreign trade with the assistance of the manufacturing sector. Or it can be done internally. Within the productive sector there can be greater production of food and reduced mining. In either case, the agricultural sector winds up with $2105 inputs. Because of the increase in productivity, inputs reproduce more than 100%. Output is $4422 rather than $4210. The additional $212 agricultural goods produced arises because of the employment of modern agricultural methods. Production in the agricultural sector generates a surplus of $2211, which is the new rent owed. This is precisely the sum of money held by the productive sector. Rent payments, production and consumption will bring us to:

Productive Class	Proprietors	Manufacturing Class
$4422 food and	$2211 money	$ 421 mfg'd goods
raw materials		

Circulation and production can continue year after year along these lines. Each year output and surpluses continue to grow. Inputs will find their way to the class which needs them. Workers will move to the sector needing them. Money will flow into the country to pay the higher rents. Reproduction with growth thus takes place according to the principles laid down by Quesnay.

The case of economic decline follows a similar pattern. As before, each class begins with the following holdings:

Productive Class	*Proprietors*	*Manufacturing Class*
$3000 food	$2000 money	$2000 mfg'd goods
$1000 raw materials		

The proprietors spend 3/5 of their incomes on manufactured goods and 2/5 on food. When other classes do likewise, this will result in the production of $3368 agricultural goods and $2211 manufactured goods in the next period. We will see how circulation, exchange, population changes, and productivity changes in agriculture generate this result. When proprietors spend their 3/5 of their income on manufactured goods and 3/5 on food we get:

Productive Class	*Proprietors*	*Manufacturing Class*
$2200 food	$ 800 food	$ 800 mfg'd goods
$1000 raw materials	$1200 mfg'd goods	$1200 money
$ 800 money		

The manufacturing class purchases $884 food from the agricultural class, representing one portion of the *Tableau*'s zig-zags. This results in:

Productive Class	*Proprietors*	*Manufacturing Class*
$1316 food	$ 800 food	$ 800 mfg'd goods
$1000 raw materials	$1200 mfg'd goods	$ 316 money
$1684 money		$ 884 food

The manufacturing sector purchases $316 manufactured goods from abroad. There is no return sale, so a trade deficit results. The deficit is necessary to meet the greater demand for manufactured goods of the agricultural class. Also, it reduces the domestic money supply by the amount that the agricultural surplus will be reduced, so in future periods the money supply will be just sufficient to facilitate domestic exchanges. This transaction makes class holdings:

Productive Class	*Proprietors*	*Manufacturing Class*
$1316 food	$ 800 food	$1116 mfg'd goods
$1000 raw materials	$1200 mfg'd goods	$ 884 food
$1684 money		

The manufacturing class sells $1011 manufactured goods to the productive class. This completes the *Tableau*'s zig-zags, and gives us:

Productive Class	Proprietors	Manufacturing Class
$1316 food	$ 800 food	$ 105 mfg'd goods
$1000 raw materials	$1200 mfg'd goods	$ 884 food
$ 673 money		$1011 money
$1011 mfg'd goods		

We now consider the effect of these expenditures on the population. The new spending propensities will result in the shift of people and their means of subsistence from agriculture to manufacturing. As we have seen, $211 in inputs must move from the agricultural sector to the manufacturing sector. To keep the number of steps involved to a minimum, I will assume that this is done in the form of $105.5 manufactured goods and $105.5 food. This migration makes holdings:

Productive Class	Proprietors	Manufacturing Class
$1210.5 food	$ 800 food	$ 210.5 mfg'd goods
$1000 raw materials	$1200 mfg'd goods	$ 989.5 food
$ 673 money		$1011 money
$ 905.5 mfg'd goods		

At this point the manufacturing sector purchases raw materials from the productive class. It needs to purchase $1011 raw materials. If the productive sector produced more raw materials and less food in the preceding period this would be possible. If not, the manufacturing class can purchase $1000 raw materials and $11 food, and obtain additional raw materials by foreign trade. Since we show the productive class with only $1000 raw materials, we will proceed in accord with the latter set of exchanges. This results in:

Productive Class	Proprietors	Manufacturing Class
$1199.5 food	$ 800 food	$ 210.5 mfg'd goods
$1684 money	$1200 mfg'd goods	$1000.5 food
$ 905.5 mfg'd goods		$1000 raw materials

The manufacturing sector exports $447.75 food, and imports $105.5 raw materials and $342.25 manufactured goods. This gives us:

Productive Class	Proprietors	Manufacturing Class
$1199.5 food	$ 800 food	$ 552.75 mfg'd goods
$1684 money	$1200 mfg'd goods	$ 552.75 food
$ 905.5 mfg'd goods		$1105.5 raw
		materials

The manufacturing sector now has the correct inputs to produce $2211 manufactured goods. The agricultural sector has $2105 of inputs. However, given Quesnay's input-output assumption, equal amounts of food and manufactured goods must be employed when producing agricultural goods. $194 food is thus wasted and goes to produce no agricultural goods. Inputs of $1811—$905.5 food and $905.5 manufactured goods produce $3368 agricultural goods rather than $3622. Advances no longer reproduce 100%. The transfer of men and capital to the manufacturing sector has lowered productivity in agriculture. Advances reproduce only 86%. Rent payments, production, and consumption finally bring us to:

Productive Class	Proprietors	Manufacturing Class
$3368 food and	$1684 money	$2211 mfg'd goods
raw materials		

The first cycle of decline is complete. Exchange and production can continue each year along these lines. Each year output, surpluses, and proprietor revenues will fall. Inputs will find their way to the class which needs them. More workers will find employment in the manufacturing sector, and agricultural productivity will continue to decline. Economic decline will occur following the schema laid out by Quesnay.

Since Quesnay worked in terms of zig-zags it is doubtful he saw the *Tableau*, even intuitively, in terms of the above circulation and production steps. The mechanisms employed above, however, are all Quesnay's. Indeed, for Quesnay population was a function of demand, and productivity in agriculture was a function of capital. He assumed these two principles would equilibrate the *Tableau* in the dynamic cases, though he never worked out the process in detail. In particular, his greatest failure was his inability to recognize the problems inherent in maintaining both that output was a function of demand and that it was function of inputs.

Since he grasped so much it would be niggling to fault Quesnay for this oversight. This is all the more true because the error has appeared again and again in attempts to reconstruct the dynamic *Tableau.*

CHAPTER V
INPUT-OUTPUT ANALYSIS AND THE *TABLEAU*

A very different means of viewing the Tableau was first suggested by Wassily Leontief. *The Structure of The American Economy, 1919-1929* opens with Leontief acknowledging his indebtedness to Quesnay and expressing recognition of the relationship between his input-output analysis and Quesnay's *Tableau*. Leontief than goes even further, claiming that he is, in fact, constructing "a *Tableau Économique* of the United States for 1919 and 1929."[117] Leontief has not been alone in noting similarities between the *Tableau* and input-output analysis. Joseph Schumpeter has remarked that "the great work of Leontief, which, entirely different though it is from Quesnay's in purpose and technique, nevertheless revived the fundamental principle of the *Tableau* method."[118]

If, in fact, Leontief and Schumpeter are correct, we should be able to use input-output techniques to illuminate the workings of the *Tableau*. A first such attempt was made by Almarin Phillips in 1955.[119] Inspired by Phillips' paper, a number of works in the history of economic thought have relied primarily or exclusively on input-output tables to explain Quesnay's model. For example, Mark Blaug's discussion of Physiocracy in *Economic Theory in Retrospect*[120] presents Quesnay's formula from "The Analysis" along with a description of the circular process depicted by it. This is then followed by a presentation of the *Tableau* as a Leontief input-output system. At no place does Blaug either present or attempt to explain the zig-zags which appear in the *Tableau*. In a similar vein, G.L.S. Shackle devotes an entire chapter of *The Years of High*

---

[117] Wassily Leontief, *The Structure of the American Economy, 1919-1929* (Cambridge: Harvard University press, 1941), p.2.

[118] Joseph A. Schumpeter, *History of Economic Analysis* (New York: Oxford University Press, 1954), pp. 241-2.

[119] Almarin Phillips, "The *Tableau Économique* as a Simple Leontief Model," *Quarterly Journal of Economics*, LXIX (Feb. 1955), 137-144.

[120] Mark Blaug, *Economic Theory in Retrospect*, 3rd edition (Cambridge: Cambridge University Press, 1978), pp. 24-29.

Theory to "Leontief's Tableau Économique."[121]   Shackle's
emphasis is on Leontief's input-output analysis, and how the *Tableau*
can be put into an input-output framework.   Again, there is no
discussion of the zig-zags; nor is there discussion of the sort of model
that is being cast into input-output tables.

It is not difficult to discern why one might think of the
Tableau as an input-output analysis for the 18th century French
economy.   There are a number of striking similarities between the
two models.   Both stress the interdependence of different economic
sectors.   According to the *Tableau,* the incomes received by the
producing classes depend upon the spending of the proprietors, while
proprietary incomes are a function of the surplus generated by the
agricultural class employing inputs from all producing sectors.   In a
Leontief system, an increase in demand by households for the
commodity produced in one industry, in turn, increases demand for
all commodities used as inputs in that industry. And greater demand
for these input commodities increases demand for the inputs used to
produce them.   All sectors of the economy are interrelated in the
sense that if we produce more of one good we have to produce more
of each of its inputs, each input to its inputs, etc.

Input-output analysis also *appears* to have all the features of
Quesnay's model—sectors, inputs, outputs, and expenditures. Most
important and most striking is that both models depend upon
technological assumptions about the necessary relations between
inputs and outputs.   We saw in Chapters II and III that Quesnay's
Tableau was constructed on the basis of certain input-output
assumptions.   Certain quantities of food and manufactured goods
yielded an output of agricultural goods which was twice the value of
the inputs used.   In the manufacturing sector Quesnay made the
assumption that no surplus was created.   This sector was thus
"sterile." A similar assumption that certain combinations of inputs
are necessary to yield an output of one unit of some commodity
provides the foundation of input-output analysis. Clearly then, there
is some resemblance between Leontief's input-output analysis and
Quesnay's *Tableau Économique.* The main questions which concern
us in this chapter are whether these resemblances are superficial or
significant ones, and whether the more sophisticated mathematics of

---

[121] G.L.S. Shackle, *The Years of High Theory* (Cambridge: Cambridge University
Press, 1967), pp. 272-285.

input-output analysis can help us better understand Quesnay's *Tableau*. It is to these issues that we now turn.

We will begin by looking at two reconstructions of the static *Tableau* based upon input-output analysis. First we look at Phillips' famous 1955 *QJE* article. Since most other input-output reconstructions—for example Blaug's and Shackle's—essentially repeat the analysis of Phillips, looking at Phillips' paper will be sufficient for understanding this approach to the *Tableau*. This will be done in Section I. Next, Section II considers a recent paper by Barna[122] which attempts to extend the simple Phillips model so that it more clearly replicates the complexity of the *Tableau*. Both papers will be subject to critical analysis in Section III. We will see here whether input-output reconstructions can be faithful to Quesnay and whether they shed any light on the workings of the *Tableau*. Finally, Section IV considers the possible use of input-output analysis to explain the dynamic *Tableau*.

SECTION I

Phillips begin his paper "The *Tableau Économique* as a Simple Leontief Model" by noting that Quesnay's zig-zags are "difficult to interpret."[123]   As a consequence, he focuses on explaining the simpler formula. It is this version of the *Tableau* that Phillips converts into a closed, three-industry Leontief model. Figure #5-1 reproduces Phillips' conversion of *Tableau* into an input-output table.[124]

Figure #5-1 is a matrix of horizontal rows and vertical columns. The rows of the matrix show the value of output for each sector and how that value is distributed throughout the economy. Thus row 1 shows that the farmers of the agricultural sector produce 4 billion in the course of a year. One billion they keep for themselves, to be used as seed and food for agriculture workers. A

---

[122] Tibor Barna, "Quesnay's *Tableau* in Modern Guise," *Economic Journal*, 85 (Sept. 1975), 485-496.

[123] Phillips, The *Tableau Économique* as a Simple Leontief Model," p. 139

[124] Phillips, "The *Tableau Économique*," p. 141 Figure #5-1 differs from Phillips' table II by excluding 1 billion food as an input into agricultural sector production. In both the *Tableau* and Phillips' input-output table this is supposed to represent interest goods, or corn which the farmer saves for bad harvest years. I have followed the policy in this work of excluding interest goods from the agricultural sector. This, I think, makes it clearer that in the agricultural sector inputs reproduce 100%.

FIGURE #5-1

TRANSACTIONS TABLE FOR THE *TABLEAU ÉCONOMIQUE*
(value of real goods in billions)

PURCHASING INDUSTRY

		I- Farmers	II- Proprietors	III- Artisans	Total Production
PRODUCING INDUSTRY	I- Farmers	1	1	2	4
	II- Proprietors	2	0	0	2
	III- Artisans	1	1	0	2
	Total Purchases	4	2	2	

second billion is bought by the proprietors, and the final 2 billion produced is purchased by the manufacturing sector. The columns of Figure #5-1 show the value of inputs received by each sector and where those inputs come from.   Column 1 shows that the agricultural sector receives 1 billion of agricultural goods from itself. This comprises the seed and food that farmers will use to produce next year's harvest. Farmers also receive 1 billion of manufactured goods from the manufacturing sector. This represents the shelter, clothes, and tools that agricultural workers will need.   Finally, farmers receive 2 billion of "rental services" from the proprietary class. Total inputs into the productive sector are thus equal to 4 billion, which is also the total production, or output, of this sector.

It is possible to view Figure #5-1 in terms of quantities rather than prices. The disadvantage of doing this is that the bottom line of the table—"total purchases"—makes no sense, since we cannot add up quantities of different goods and get a meaningful figure. This same point holds true of the *Tableau.* Quesnay's versions of the *Tableau* were all in terms of prices or values, and reconstructions of the *Tableau* have been done in value terms.   Of course, these could have been done as well in quantity terms. The easiest way to make this transformation would be to let the price of one unit of all goods be equal to $1. This would give us reconstructions of the *Tableau* in quantity terms. The disadvantage of doing this (unless we assume that all prices are constant, in which case we are again essentially talking in value terms) is that we get no figures for total output for the economy. Thus when we are interested in growing or declining economies—as we were in Chapter IV, and as we will be again in Chapter VI—we have no measure to determine whether total output has changed, and if so, in which direction.

After setting forth his input-output table, Phillips proceeds by deriving its input-output coefficients. These represent input requirements per dollar of output. As column 1 shows, each billion dollars of agricultural goods produced require 1/2 its inputs from the proprietors, and 1/4 of its inputs from each of the 2 producing classes. Input-output coefficients for all 3 sectors are given below in the rectangular matrix α.

$$\alpha = \begin{bmatrix} .25 & .5 & 1 \\ .5 & 0 & 0 \\ .25 & .5 & 0 \end{bmatrix}$$

Alpha is what Leontief calls a structural matrix of the economy.[125] Each row of α shows output coefficients, or where the output of each sector goes on a proportional basis. Each column of α shows input coefficients, or the combination of inputs necessary to produce \$1 billion of goods.

A 3 industry Leontief system is a system of simultaneous equations of the form:

$$\begin{array}{rcll} (1-a_{11})X_1 & -a_{12}X_2 & -a_{13}X_3 & = & 0 \\ -a_{21}X_1 + (1-a_{22})X_2 & -a_{23}X_3 & = & 0 \\ -a_{31}X_1 & -a_{32}X2 + (1-a_{33})X_3 & = & 0 \end{array}$$

where X_i, is the output of the i-th sector and a_{ij} is the input-output coefficient. Substitution of input-output coefficients from α yields no unique solution. But any solution must be such that $X_1 = 2X_2 = 2X_3$. That is, Quesnay's system requires that the value of output from the productive, proprietary, and manufacturing classes be in the ratio 2:1:1. The figures that we used in Chapter III—agriculture

[125] Wassily Leontief, *Input-Output Economics* (New York: Oxford University Press, 1966), p. 15.

output of $4000, proprietor rents of $2000, and manufacturing output of $2000—is such a ratio, and hence a solution to the Leontief equations.

There are several preliminary objections to Phillips' input-output reconstruction that warrant making at this point. First Figure #5-1 fails to show the role of foreign trade in the *Tableau*. This shortcoming is understandable. Phillips' paper appeared in 1955. This was several years before the publication of Ronald Meek's paper "Problems of the *Tableau Économique*"[126] which demonstrated the critical role of foreign trade in the *Tableau*. Next Phillips' 3 x 3 matrix fails to disaggregate agricultural goods into food and raw material. Since Quesnay made definite assumptions about both raw material and food inputs in manufacturing sector production, these assumptions should be made clear in an input-output table, not disguised by aggregation. Third, according to Figure #5-1 artisans use only agricultural inputs to produce manufactured goods; no manufactured goods are assumed to be needed. Quesnay's zig-zags, which show artisans of the manufacturing sector spending half their money receipts on agricultural goods and the other half within the manufacturing sector on manufactured goods, are thus ignored.

These preliminary objections can be dealt with by expanding and amending the simple 3 X 3 Phillips matrix.[127] First, import and export sectors will be introduced. This is done in Figure #5-2 below. Note that now 1/2 billion of agricultural goods is exported and 1/2 billion (of manufactured goods) in imported. This is consistent with the reconstruction of the static *Tableau* in Chapter III, and with Quesnay's views on foreign trade. I have also changed the column heading from "purchasing industry" to "consuming industry" in the interest of clarity. As we saw in Chapter III, the manufacturing sector *purchases* $2 billion or $2000 of agricultural goods. However, one-quarter of this is not consumed, but exported for an equal value of manufactured goods.

Figure #5-3 goes one step further and disaggregates the productive sector into 2 different sectors—the first a mining sector producing raw materials, and the second a farming sector producing

---

[126] Meek's paper appeared in *Economica* in November 1960. It is reprinted in Meek, *Economics of Physiocracy*, pp. 265-296.

[127] Expansion of the 3 X 3 Phillips' matrix has also been attempted by Barna, "Quesnay's *Tableau* in Modern Guise." Barna's reconstruction is treated later in this chapter.

FIGURE #5-2

TRANSACTION TABLE FOR THE *TABLEAU ÉCONOMIQUE*

(value of real goods in billions)

CONSUMING INDUSTRY

PRODUCING INDUSTRY		I- Productive Sector	II- Proprietors	III- Mfg. Sector	IV- Exports	Total Prod.
	I- Farmers	1	1	1½	½	4
	II- Proprietors	2	0	0	0	2
	III-Artisans	1	1	0	0	2
	IV-Imports Mfg'd Goods	1	1	½	0	½
	Total Purchases	4	2	2	½	

FIGURE #5-3

TRANSACTIONS TABLE FOR THE *TABLEAU ÉCONOMIQUE*

(value of real goods in billions)

CONSUMING INDUSTRY

PRODUCING INDUSTRY		I-Food	II- Raw Materials	IV- Proprietors	V- Artisans	VI- Exports	Total Demand
	I-Food	¾	¼	1	½	½	3
	II-Raw Materials	0	0	0	1	0	1
	III- Proprietors	1½	½	0	0	0	2
	IV- Mfg.	¾	¼	1	0	0	2
	V-Imports (mfg.)	0	0	0	½	0	½
		3	1	2	2	½	

food. Disaggregating the prductive sector in this manner allows a clearer demonstration of Quesnay's input-output assumptions by means of a Leontief input-output table. Figures #5-1 and #5-2 are insufficient for this purpose. The manufacturing sector should produce $2 billion of manufactured goods using $1 billion raw materials and 1/2 billion each of manufactured goods and food. By aggregating the raw materials and food produced within the productive sector, Phillips' simple 3 X 3 matrix is unable to show the full input-output assumptions that lie behind manufacturing sector production. By disaggregating the productive sector we bring Phillips' reconstruction of the *Tableau* into greater conformity with the terminology of the *Tableau* and make clear all of its input-output relations.   In constructing Figure #5-3, I have assumed that Quesnay's input-output assumptions for the productive sector were true of both mining and farming. Thus the mining and farming sectors each use $X billion of food and $X billion of manufacturedgoods to produce $4X billion of output. The difference between the value of inputs and the value of output for each sector is that sector's surplus. This is paid to the proprietors, as before.

Figure #5-3 yields the following structural matrix of input-output coefficients:

$$\beta = \begin{bmatrix} .25 & .25 & .5 & .25 & 1 \\ 0 & 0 & 0 & .5 & 0 \\ .5 & .5 & 0 & 0 & 0 \\ .25 & .25 & .5 & 0 & 0 \\ 0 & 0 & 0 & .25 & 0 \end{bmatrix}$$

Our Leontief system consists of the following 5 equations:

$$
\begin{aligned}
(1-a_{11})X_1 & -a_{12}X_2 & -a_{13}X_3 & -a_{14}X_4 & -a_{15}X_5 & = 0 \\
-a_{21}X_1 & +(1-a_{22})X_2 & -a_{23}X_3 & -a_{24}X_4 & -a_{25}X_5 & = 0 \\
-a_{31}X_1 & -a_{32}X_2 & +(1-a_{33})X_3 & -a_{34}X_4 & -a_{35}X_5 & = 0 \\
-a_{41}X_1 & -a_{42}X_2 & -a_{43}X_3 & +(1-a_{44})X_4 & -a_{45}X_5 & = 0 \\
-a_{51}X_1 & -a_{52}X_2 & -a_{53}X_3 & -a_{54}X_4 & +(1-a_{55})X_5 & = 0
\end{aligned}
$$

Substituting from the structural matrix β, we have 5 equations:

$$
\begin{aligned}
.75X_1 & -.25X_2 & -.5X_3 & -.25X_4 & -X_5 & = 0 \\
& X_2 & & -.5X_4 & & = 0 \\
-.5X_1 & -.5X_2 & +X_3 & & & = 0 \\
-.25X_1 & -.25X_2 & -.5X_3 & +X_4 & & = 0 \\
& & & -.25X_4 & +X_5 & = 0
\end{aligned}
$$

and 5 unknowns—the output, X_i, from each of our 5 sectors. Only 4 equations are linearly independent, so we cannot solve for absolute levels of output for each sector. The best we can do is derive relative levels of output: $X_1 = 3X_2 = 1.5X_3 = 1.5X_4 = 6X_5$. This means that the output of food (X_1) must be three times the output of raw materials (X_2), one-and-a-half times the output of proprietor rental services (X_3), one-and-a-half times the output of manufactured goods from the manufacturing sector (X_4), and 6 times the imports of foreign manufactured goods (X_5). There is no unique solution to this system. Any solution will represent an economy that is able to reproduce itself from year to year because output is just sufficient to provide the inputs so that same output can be produced again. One solution set is the figures under the total demand column in Figure #5-3. An economy producing $3 billion food, $1 billion of raw materials, $2 billion apiece of rental services and manufactured goods, and which imports $1/2 billion of manufactured goods will be able to reproduce itself. The exchanges that are necessary to get inputs into the proper sector are shown by the individual boxes of Figure #5-3.[128] When all the transactions have taken place, each sector is in possession of the inputs necessary for it to produce the same input it produced in the preceding year. Production can now take place and the economy reproduces itself.

SECTION II

Before examining some more serious objections to input-put reconstructions of the *Tableau* we will look at a second presentation of the *Tableau* in input-output format. Barna has expanded Phillips' 3 X 3 matrix into a 9 X 9 input-output table in order to show all the *Tableau*'s reproduction relations.[129] This table is reproduced as Figure #5-4.[130]

To derive Figure #5-4 from Figure #5-1 several additions to Phillips' matrix must be made. First, foreign trade has again been incorporated into the model by adding separate export and import sectors. $263 billion of food is exported (shown in row 1, column 9) and $263 billion of manufactured goods is imported (shown in row 9, column 2). Next, a separate sector is added for capital consump-

---

[128] We ignore for now the question of these exchanges having a required order or sequence.

[129] Barna,"Quesnay's *Tableau* in Modern Guise."

[130] Ibid., p. 488

FIGURE #5-4

SOCIAL ACCOUNTING MATRIX OF TRANSACTIONS

| | Industries Current a/c | | Capital a/c | Households | | | | | Foreign countries | |
	Agric. (1)	Non-agric. (2)	Agric. (3)	Farm (4)	Artisan (5)	Land-lord (6)	State (7)	Church (8)	Exports (9)	Total
(1) Agricultural produce	525	525	525	525	263	300	150	75	263	3150
(2) Manufactures	...	...	...	525	263	300	150	75	...	1313
(3) Capital consumption	525	...	...	...	...	...	...	.	...	525
(4) Farm incomes	1050	...	...	...	...	...	...	...	...	1050
(5) Non-farm incomes	...	525	...	...	...	...	...	...	...	525
(6) Rent	1050	...	...	...	...	...	...	...	...	1050
(7) Taxes	...	...	...	...	...	300	...	...	...	300
(8) Tithes	...	...	...	...	...	150	...	...	...	150
(9) Imports	...	...	...	...	...	...	...	...	...	263
Total	3150	1313	525	1050	525	1050	300	150	263	8325
Working capital	1050	525								
Fixed Capital	4333	2000								

Source: "Third edition" of *Tableau économique*   Note: Figures may not add exactly due to rounding errors.

tion and replenishment.[131]   The figure in row 1, column 3 shows the amount of agricultural goods that are produced for replacing capital used up in the production process; and the figure in row 3, column 1 shows the amount of capital used up in production. In a static economy, depreciation will equal capital replacements.

Barna also adds rows and columns that show receipts and expenditures by the church and by the state. This disaggregates Quesnay's proprietary sector into three classes. Revenues accruing to the church and state come from payments by the landlords. Landlords pay taxes to the state and tithes to the church. All previous reconstructions have aggregated the landlords, the church, and the state into one sector called "proprietors." Since all 3 classes function similarly, Barna has assumed that receipts of the 3 classes are used in the same manner. Taxes and tithes are thus spent in equal proportions on food and manufactured goods. State spending is shown in column 7 and church spending is shown in column 8. Finally, Barna attempts to distinguish means of production from means of consumption. Means of consumption are inputs going to sustain workers. Means of production are inputs used by workers in producing goods.   Food, shelter, and clothing are means of consumption; seed, barns, and tools are means of production. There is some evidence for such a distinction in Quesnay. For example, in the first edition of the *Tableau* Quesnay maintains that one-half of agricultural costs of production comprise the wage labor of men.[132] It follows that the other half must be for seed and other items necessary for production.

By disaggregating inputs of the 2 producing sectors we get 2 additional producing sectors and 2 additional consuming sectors. The additional consuming sectors are farm and artisan households (columns 4 and 5 respectively). These receive wages or means of consumption. Barna calls the additional producing sectors "farm incomes" and "non-farm incomes" (rows 4 and 5 respectively). These terms are in some sense misnomers because incomes are not *produced* by agricultural and manufacturing sector workers. Incomes are *spent* by households. What is produced or sold is labor

---

[131] This is the second billion of food that Phillips includes as an input for the agricultural sector. (See footnote #124). It is an easy matter to remove depreciation and replenishment of capital from Barna's table. All we need to do is eliminate column 3 and row 3.

[132] Meek, *Economics of Physiocracy*, p. 110

power—farm labor power and non-farm labor power.

Of greater importance, is the fact that it is not clear how where the numerical values in Figure #5-4 were derived, or on what assumptions they are based. Barna maintains that his source is the third edition of the *Tableau*, translated by Kuczynski and Meek in *Quesnay's Tableau Économique*. Kuczynski and Meek's third edition though has a base of 600. The value of manufactured goods produced, proprietor rents, and agricultural inputs then should each be 600.[133] Abstracting from capital consumption, church, and state, as Quesnay does, proprietor rents and spending falls from 1060 to 600. But manufacturing output according to Figure #5-4 is 1313. Excluding church and state as consumers of manufactured goods reduces manufacturing output to only 1088. Meanwhile, agricultural output less state, church, and capital consumption is 2138. These figures do not constitute a solution to the set of equations that represent the *Tableau*. We saw earlier that agriculture output must be twice manufacturing output, and we have seen that Quesnay maintained that the proprietors' rents must equal the agricultural surplus, which is equal to half the value of agricultural inputs. Finally, Barna seems to misconstrue Quesnay's input-output assumption. In the productive sector, it is assumed that no means of production are purchased from the manufacturing sector.[134] This is represented by the dash in row 2, column 1. Manufacturing sector inputs come from 3 sources: (1) the agricultural sector, in the form of 525 raw materials and food; (2) imports of 263 manufactured goods; and (3) non-farm labor power, which is maintained according to column 5 by 263 food and 263 manufactured goods. The value of manufactured inputs is thus 525[135] while the output of manufactured goods is valued at 1313. We saw earlier however that

---

[133] Barna, "Quesnay's *Tableau* in Modern Guise," p. 490, correctly points out that the elimination of church and state reduces initial demand by 3/7, so all other transactions will be 3/7 less. Therefore, to convert Figure #5-4 into an input-output version of the *Tableau* it is necessary to reduce all other entries by 3/7 when rows 7 and 8 and, columns 7 and 8, are deleted. The problem however, remains that the *ratios* between agricultural output, manufacturing output, and rent are incorrect. Reducing everything by 3/7 will not solve this problem. Moreover, reducing manufacturing output by 3/7 gives us 622 manufactured goods, and reducing agricultural output by 3/7 yields 1216 agricultural goods. These figures cannot be right, and are not the figures of the third edition of the *Tableau*.

[134] Ibid., p. 490

[135] We get 525 rather than 526 because of rounding errors.

manufactured goods should constitute 1/4 the value of inputs used in producing manufactured goods. Barna's input-output assumptions are then not those of Quesnay.

With only a few alterations, however, it is possible to convert Figure #5-4 into a matrix consistent with Quesnay's input-output assumptions. This is done in Figure #5-5, a 6 X 6 input-output table with a base of $2000. Deleting the columns and rows for capital con-

FIGURE #5-5

SOCIAL ACCOUNTING MATRIX OF TRANSACTIONS

	agric. industry	mfg. industry	landlord household	farm household	artisan household	exports	Total Demand
agriculture	500	1250	1000	500	250	500	4000
manufacturing	500	0	1000	500	0	0	2000
proprietors	2000	0	0	0	0	0	2000
farm income	1000	0	0	0	0	0	1000
mfg. income	0	500	0	0	0	0	500
imports (mfg)	0	250	0	0	250	0	
TOTAL	4000	2000	2000	1000	500	500	

sumption, for the church, and for the state has enabled me to condense Barna's matrix into a more manageable 6 X 6 table. This is justified since all classes spend their incomes in the same fashion. In addition, inputs for the 2 producing sectors are split 50-50 between means of production for the industry and means of subsistence for those working in industry. We now find that agricultural goods are produced using $500 agricultural goods (seed), $500 manufactured goods (tools), and $1000 of labor power or "farm income". This income is spent by farm households. Column 4 shows how farm households spend their income. Half is spent on manufactured goods (clothing and shelter) and the other half on agricultural goods (food).   Total agricultural inputs are $1000 agricultural goods and $1000 manufactured goods. Manufactured goods are produced using $1250 agricultural goods ($1000 raw materials + $250 food), $250 manufactured imports, and $500 "artisan income."   Column 5 shows that artisans spend half their income on agricultural goods (food) and half their income on manufactured goods (clothing and shelter).   This makes total manufacturing inputs $1000 raw materials, $500 food, and $500 manufactured goods. These are the same figures from our solution to the static *Tableau* in Chapter III.

Figure #5-5 can easily be converted into a structural matrix whose input-output coefficients can be used to solve for the output of each sector. Gamma, γ, is the structural matrix derived from Figure #5-5:

$$\gamma = \begin{bmatrix} .125 & .625 & .5 & .5 & .5 & 1 \\ .125 & 0 & .5 & .5 & 0 & 0 \\ .5 & 0 & 0 & 0 & 0 & 0 \\ .25 & 0 & 0 & 0 & 0 & 0 \\ 0 & .25 & 0 & 0 & 0 & 0 \\ 0 & .125 & 0 & 0 & .5 & 0 \end{bmatrix}$$

Gamma gives us the following set of 6 linear equations:

$$
\begin{array}{lllllll}
.875X_1 & -.625X_2 & -.5X_3 & -.5X_4 & -.5X_5 & -X_6 & = 0 \\
-.125X_1 & + X_2 & -.5X_3 & -.5X_4 & & & = 0 \\
-.5X_1 & & + X_3 & & & & = 0 \\
-.25X_1 & & & + X_4 & & & = 0 \\
& -.25X_2 & & & + X_5 & & = 0 \\
& -.125X_2 & & & -.5X_5 & +X_6 & = 0
\end{array}
$$

whose solution set is $.5X_1 = X_2 = X_3 = 2X_4 = 4X_5 = 4X_6$. One set of figures satisfying this criterion is the total demand column of Figure #5-5. Thus we saw in Chapter III, a solution to the *Tableau* involves production of $4000 agricultural good, $2000 manufactured goods, $2000 in proprietor rents, and $500 worth of manufactured imports.

SECTION III

Having examined the superficial criticisms of input-output reconstructions we turn to the more serious objections to this approach. In particular, we will examine what the above input-output analyses demonstrate, and what they fail to show.

What is demonstrated by the solutions to the input-output tables represented by Figure #5-3 and Figure #5-5 is that Quesnay's system is complete or feasible. That is, it shows that outputs from all sectors are sufficient to provide the required inputs into the various sectors of the economy so that the same outputs can be reproduced. This establishes a necessary condition for an economy to reproduce, and is not a result that should be dismissed lightly. For we have seen time and again the inability of commentators on the *Tableau* to demonstrate just this fact. Even the analyses of Phillips and Barna in Sections I and II failed in this respect.

On the other hand, proof of the consistency of Quesnay's assumptions is not the same as an explanation of Quesnay's model. Nor does it show that reproduction indeed will take place if these input-output assumptions are met. For this more ambitious task we need a set of *necessary and sufficient* conditions. Input-output reconstructions do not attempt this more ambitious undertaking.

A complete as well as consistent explanation of Quesnay's model, or, a set of necessary *and* sufficient conditions for reproduction would require three additional things: (1) an analysis of the role of money in the *Tableau*, (2) an analysis of the exchange relations of the model, and (3) a further analysis of the foreign trade assumption Quesnay employs.[136]

Quesnay was not interested in describing a barter economy. The *Tableau* describes an economy in which buying and selling is done with money. That is why all numbers in the *Tableau* are given in monetary figures rather than in quantities. If an economy possessed no money, or if it had an insufficient quantity of money, then despite the fact that the economy *could* reproduce, it *would not* do so. Let us consider an economy with a base of $2000, as described in Chapter III or depicted in Figure #5-5. However, let the supply of money be $1000 rather than $2000. This creates an

---

[136] Conditions (1) and (2) are obviously related. An analysis of money will be, in part an analysis of how money functions in exchange.

immediate problem. If the proprietors begin with only $1000 and
spend half of this sum of food and the other half of manufactured
goods, when all the zig-zags transactions have been completed, output in both producing sectors will be half as great as before. From
the vantage point of the input-output analysis, however, there is no
problem here; nor does output decline when considering this
situation. The old output—*Tableau* with a base of $2000—is still a
possible solution.

Money does not matter for an input-output table. But money
mattered to Quesnay. He was very careful in trying to estimate the
quantity of money in the economy and show that this quantity was
sufficient to enable reproduction to take place. It was not enough for
Quesnay that the manufacturing sector needed agricultural goods
and the agricultural sector needed manufactured goods. In a barter
economy the two sectors could barter for what each needed. But in
a monetary economy if one sector wants goods produced by another
sector it must have the wherewithal to purchase these goods. At the
outset, when we begin our analysis, it is arbitrary who holds the
money. But the money must be sufficient for this sector to purchase
the inputs it needs. And this transaction must put sufficient money
into the hands of the other sectors so that they too may purchase the
commodities they require. Only if every sector has the money to
purchase the inputs it requires will the economy be able to reproduce
last year's output. This crucial role of money was recognized by
Quesnay, and he realized that money and money flows had to be
represented in his model. This, of course, was the whole point of the
zig-zags. Input-output reconstructions of the *Tableau* unfortunately,
abstract from a salient feature of Quesnay's model. As a consequence, it is not clear how much illumination they can really throw
on Quesnay's model.

Barna[137] has argued that the simultaneous solution to the
Tableau provided by input-output analysis is superior to the "iterative
solution" of Quesnay's zig-zags and Meek's tables. Both provide
solutions to Quesnay's system of economic circulation and
production; however, according to Barna, there are two difficulties
with the iterative solution. An iterative process of computations may
be confused with a dynamic process through time. But the two,
Barna argues, are not the same.   For an iterative process of

---

[137] Barna, "Quesnay's *Tableau* in Modern Guise," p. 495.

computations may converge towards a solution in diminishing steps. In addition, the order of the steps in the iterative process may suggest the existence of time lags, or that some of the steps may be ordered in a certain way. But, Barna continues, "the order of the steps is arbitrary since the starting point of the computations is arbitrary."[138]

Neither of these arguments is very good. An explanation of the *Tableau* should be capable of showing a dynamic process through time. For this is what the *Tableau* is really about. Chapter IV showed this to be possible using "an iterative solution." In the next section of this chapter, I will show this to be beyond the capabilities of input-output analysis.

Barna's second argument, that the order of the sequence is arbitrary (since the starting point of the computation is arbitrary), is a fallacious one. A simple mathematical example can perhaps best make this point. Consider the sequence 1, 2, 3, 4, 5, 1, 2, 3, 4, 5, 1, 2, 3, 4, 5,... Any place that we break into or begin the sequence is arbitrary. But not so the order of the sequence. If we break in at 3, the next step must be 4. Then the step after 4 must be 5. There is nothing arbitrary about 4 following 3 and 5 following 4.

The same holds true of the exchange relations in Quesnay's *Tableau*. We can begin anywhere in the circular flow process. But one we have chosen a starting point it does not follow that the next step is arbitrary. Only certain steps will be possible. Consider again the first step involved in reconstructing the static *Tableau* in Section V of Chapter III. The manufacturing sector holds $2000 manufactured goods, and the agricultural sector holds $2000 in money, $1000 raw materials, and $3000 food. The proprietors have $2000 in rent claims, equal to the surplus of the just completed production period. At this point the next step is not arbitrary. It *cannot* be proprietor spending, since the proprietors have no money to spend. Nor can it be the purchase of raw material by the manufacturing sector. For artisans too have no money. The productive class can buy $1000 manufactured goods at this point, but this will affect the entire sequence, since only $1000 will be left to pay rent to the proprietors. And less income for the proprietors, as we have seen, means less demand for agricultural goods and less production in succeeding years.

---

[138] Ibid., p. 495.

The steps involved in the *Tableau* are not arbitrary. They have a certain order and logic that must be adhered to. Circulation must occur in a definite sequence if production is to be maintained at the same level. Since input-output analysis provides a simultaneous solution, it cannot take any required sequence in the circulation process into account. As such, iterative solutions to the *Tableau* must be preferred to the simultaneous ones. They have greater expository power, showing more clearly and in greater detail the actual circulation process.

This point was recognized by Joseph Schumpeter. In contradistinction to Barna, Schumpeter saw that there was something crucial in the *Tableau*—a demonstration of how exchange must take place—that is lacking in input-output tables. Schumpeter writes: "in one respect [the *Tableau* is] superior to the logically more satisfactory method [i.e., input-output analysis]; it visualized the (stationary) economic process as a circuit flow that in each period returns upon itself. ...[I]t is also a method of conveying features of the [economic process]—definite sequences in particular—that do not stand out equally well in a system of simultaneous equations."[139] In a similar vein, E.K. Hunt has maintained that the money and exchange relations of the *Tableau* provide an explanation of economic crises. "The Physiocrats anticipated T.R. Malthus, Karl Marx and J.M. Keynes, and many other subsequent economist who showed how the hording of money or the development of bottlenecks or imbalances in the process of monetary circulation could disrupt the allocation of inputs and commodity outputs and create economic crises or depressions."[140] Input-output analysis, by abstracting from the process of monetary circulation thus cuts itself off from an explanation of economic decline.

The final inadequacy of input-output reconstructions has to do with foreign trade. In Chapter III we examined how all nations could export food and import manufactured goods. For this is what the *Tableau* requires. Section V of that chapter closed Quesnay's system by showing what would have to occur for the foreign trade assumption of the *Tableau* to be satisfied. The same question must be raised concerning input-output reconstructions. In Chapter III we saw one possible solution to be the existence of another nation

---

[139] Schumpeter, *History of Economic Analysis*, p. 243.

[140] E.K. Hunt, *History of Economic Thought: A Critical Perspective* (Belmont: Wadsworth, 1979), p. 32. Also see section I of chapter VI.

that produced an excess of manufactured goods. In input-output analysis this would require another input-output table. The economy represented would have to export $500 manufactured goods and import $500 food. Without seeing all the input-output relations of this economy, however, there is no assurance that an economy exporting manufactured goods and importing food is viable.

A second solution to closing the system of the *Tableau* involved a change in the composition of the population. Agricultural sector workers left their farms, seeking work in the factories and shops in the manufacturing sector. This reduced the excess food produced while also decreasing the surplus of manufactured goods. Domestic equilibrium was re-established when the population changed so that no foreign trade was necessary. But how could this second solution be represented on an input-output table, which takes no account of the population? Moreover, as we will see in the next section, input-output analysis is incapable of representing these kinds of dynamic changes.

Finally, some less objectionable but nonetheless noteworthy deficiencies of input-output reconstruction of the *Tableau* warrant mentioning. It is a fundamental tenet of Physiocracy that only the productive sector generates a net product. The manufacturing sector is "sterile"; the value of its inputs is equal to the value of manufactured goods produced. This principle—that surpluses arise exclusively in the agricultural sector—shows up in all *non*-input-output reconstructions of the *Tableau*. But how can a surplus be shown in an input-output table where by definition inputs must equal outputs for each industry?[141] Phillips shows the agricultural surplus by means of the proprietors' rent. "Only agriculture appears to produce a net produce since, by assumption, only farmers pay rent."[142] But these rent payments are also remuneration for "rental services"[143] according to Phillips. They are as such factor payments, which constitute inputs used to produce agricultural goods. On this interpretation there is no surplus, the value of the inputs and the value of agricultural output being the same. Quesnay was able to represent agricultural surpluses since he did not consider "rental services" as an input. Factors of production are irrelevant in

---

[141] Leontief, *Input-Ouput*, p. 158f. "The rows and columns—...—come into balance in the double entry bookkeeping of input-output economics." (p. 159)

[142] Phillips, "The *Tableau Économique* as a Simple Leontief Model," p. 143f.

[143] Phillips, "The *Tableau Économique* as a Simple Leontief Model," p. 141

Quesnay's model.[144]   By considering rent payments as inputs to agricultural production, input-output reconstructions pervert Quesnay's intentions.   This is surely something to be avoided, especially when there is something better available.

SECTION IV

We turn briefly now to the use of input-output analysis to explain the workings of the dynamic versions of the *Tableau.*

In a 1965 paper, "Input-Output Analysis"[145] Leontief attempted to expand and develop input-output tables into dynamic models of the economy.   Such models were necessary according to the Leontief in order to make input-output models closer to actual economic processes.

Leontief converts input-output tables into a dynamic model by introducing capital into the system of simultaneous equations that represents the production relations of an economy.   A stock of capital goods becomes a necessary input in the production process.   Increases in the stock of capital goods show the growth of an economy, and provide the requisite for further growth.   Likewise, a reduction in capital stocks shows economic decline.   The reduced capital available limits future production and the stock of capital declines further.

----

[144] "It is, of course, in Quesnay's *Tableau Économique* that it is found the original picture of the system of production and consumption as a circular process, and it stands in striking contrast to the view presented in modern theory, of a one-way avenue that leads from 'factors of production' to 'Consumption goods.'   Piero Sraffa, *Production of Commodities by Means of Commodities* (Cambridge: Cambridge University Press, 1960), p. 93.   "[The surplus] represents the extraction, by the feudal nobility, of the surplus output of the land, and the consumption of this, partly as agricultural luxury products, and partly as luxuries manufactured by the sterile class. In modern times, neoclassical historians of economic analysis have responded to the situation by a drastic expedient: that of inventing an industry for the class of proprietors to engage in, so that they may be regarded as producing landlord services and so that the revenue they receive is composed of payment for these services. This move is perfectly consistent with the assumptions of neoclassical theory, . . ., but, as the basis for an interpretation of physiocracy, it has serious problems. Thus, on this analysis the surplus disappears—indeed, one cannot even introduce the concept—and there are three industries, each producing a product for which the return just covers its opportunity cost."   Vivian Walsh and Harvey Gram, *Classical and Neoclassical Theories of General Equilibrium* (New York: Oxford University Press, 1980), pp. 36f.

[145] Reprinted in Leontief, *Input-Output Economics*, pp. 134-155.

The stock of capital goods produced by sector i which sector j must hold per unit of output is denoted by b_{ij}. Thus b_{13} represents the capital that sector 3 must obtain from sector 1 to produce 1 unit of output. Considering all industries and all fixed capital requirements, a matrix similar to λ will describe all capital requirement for the entire economy.

$$\lambda = \begin{bmatrix} b_{11} & b_{12} & . & . & . & . & b_{1n} \\ b_{21} & b_{22} & . & . & . & . & b_{2n} \\ . & . & & & & & . \\ . & . & & & & & . \\ . & . & & & & & . \\ b_{n1} & b_{n2} & . & . & . & . & b_{nn} \end{bmatrix}$$

The next step in constructing a dynamic input-output model is the dating of all inputs and outputs.

Following the standard notation of dating each year's output with superscripts and letting subscripts identify different economic sectors, we can describe a two-sector economy over a period of 3 years by the following 6 equations:[146]

$$
\begin{aligned}
(1-a_{11})X_1^1 & & -a_{12}X_2^1 & -b_{11}(X_1^2-X_1^1) & -b_{12}(X_2^2-X_2^1) &= 0 \\
-a_{21}X_1^1 & + (1-a_{22})X_2^1 & & -b_{21}(X_1^2-X_1^1) & -b_{22}(X_2^2-X_2^1) &= 0 \\
(1-a_{11})X_1^2 & & -a_{12}X_2^2 & -b_{11}(X_1^3-X_1^2) & -b_{12}(X_2^3-X_2^2) &= 0 \\
-a_{21}X_1^2 & + (1-a_{22})X_2^2 & & -b_{21}(X_1^3-X_1^2) & -b_{22}(X_2^3-X_2^2) &= 0 \\
(1-a_{11})X_1^3 & & -a_{12}X_2^3 & -b_{11}(X_1^4-X_1^3) & -b_{12}(X_2^4-X_2^3) &= 0 \\
-a_{21}X_1^3 & + (1-a_{22})X_2^3 & & -b_{21}(X_1^4-X_1^3) & -b_{22}(X_2^4-X_2^3) &= 0
\end{aligned}
$$

Output from sector 2 in year 2 (line #4) can go to any of 4 places. As in static input-output models, output is purchased and used as inputs for sector 1 or sector 2 in year 2. This is shown by the first two sums of equation 4 and is identical to the static case except for

---

[146] These equations are adapted from Leontief, *Input-Output Economics*, p.147.

the inclusion of superscripts indicating that this year's output in sector 2—X_2^2—is to be used as inputs during this year's production. $-a_{21}X_1^2$ is the output purchased by sector 1 (in year 2) and $-a_{22}X_2^2$ is the output purchased by sector 2 (in year 2). The new expressions in equation #4 represent capital accumulation. ($X_1^3 - X_1^2$) represents the change in sector 1 output between year 2 and year 3. To produce greater output will require more capital. b_{21} is the additional capital per unit output that sector 1 will need from sector 2. The total expression $-b_{21}(X_1^3 - X_1^2)$ indicates how much additional capital sector 1 will need from sector 2 to increase its output in year 3. Obviously this capital will have to come out of the current year's (year 2) output from sector 2. Similarly, sector 2 will need additional capital if it is to increase its output from X_2^2 to X_2^3. Its capital requirement for increasing output next year will be $b_{22}(X_2^3 - X_2^2)$, and this too must come out of current output from sector 2.

The 6 equations above contain 8 unknowns— the output from sectors 1 and 2 for each of the four years under consideration. We must be concerned here with four years rather than three because output in year 3 depends upon the output of year 4. To increase output in year 4 requires more capital, which must be produced in year 3. Having more unknowns than equations, the system is undetermined and not solvable. However, given the two X_j's for any year i, we can proceed to solve for the remaining X_j's. These will tell us the growth (or decline) path that the economy follows through time. If $X_j^n < X_j^{n+1}$ sector j has grown, while if the reverse is true, sector j declines.

The only attempt that has been made to incorporate the *Tableau* into a dynamic input-output framework was carried out by Barna, whose 1976 paper on "Quesnay's Model of Economic Development"[147] contains an input-output matrix representing the dynamic *Tableau* plus a mechanism which explains how capital is accumulated and how the accumulation of capital leads to further growth.

The dynamic input-output matrix is built upon Barna's static model. We have already seen the problems with Barna's static model of the *Tableau* and have made the appropriate corrections. So we will begin out extension of the model to the dynamic case from the

---

[147] Tibor Barna, "Quesnay's Model of Economic Development," *European Economic Review*, 8 (1976), 315-338.

corrected input-output table—Figure #5-5. To generate a dynamic model from Figure #5-5 two emendations are necessary. First the agricultural sector must be further disaggregated. Barna distinguishes two agricultural sectors. One he calls "traditional agriculture" and the other "modern agriculture." This disaggregation is equivalent to Quesnay's distinction between large-scale cultivation (*la grande culture*) and small-scale cultivation (*la petite culture*). The most important point concerning this distinction is that productivity is higher in the modern agricultural sector.

Barna's second addition is the introduction of a special accumulation sector. The difference between the agricultural surplus and the rent paid by that sector is profit. This goes to the farmer. If the farmer does not spend these profits on luxury consumption, but plows them back into agriculture instead, capital accumulates in the agriculture sector. Accumulated capital can then be used as an input into the production of agricultural goods in the next production period.

Figure #5-6 represents Barna's dynamic input-output model for a given year.[148] If we begin by assuming that there are no profits and no capital accumulation in agriculture, i.e., $a_{18}X_1 = a_{28}X_2 = 0$,[149] then Figure #5-6 will be virtually identical to Figure #5-5. Now let us make the model dynamic. Barna writes: "At the initial stage there must be sudden emergence of profits which are reinvested. Exogenous shock is given to the system by the implementation of the policies of laissez-faire and tax reform."[150] These reforms will increase agricultural output, given an amount of inputs. The net product likewise increases. Rents, however, are fixed in terms of the surplus that has existed in the past. An increase in the net product does not immediately increase rents by the same amount. With rents fixed, any additional surplus becomes the farm-

---

[148] This table differs significantly from Barna's model given on p. 321 of "Quesnay's Model...". The problems with Barna's table are far too numerous to detail. Several are holdovers from Barna's static input-output table. Figure #5-6 though, I believe, captures the essence of Barna's reconstruction. Since Barna provides neither numerical values nor passages in Quesnay from which numerical values can be inferred, I have used algebraic notation to represent these values in Figure #5-6.

[149] Of course, Quesnay always operates on the assumption of no profits in manufacturing—i.e., $a_{38}X_3=0$. It makes no sense to speak of profits in other sectors.

[150] Barna, "Quesnay's Model...", p. 236.

FIGURE #5-6
SOCIAL ACCOUNTING MATRIX OF TRANSACTIONS
(value of goods in billions of dollars)

	trad. agric.	modern agric.	mfg.	landlord household	farm	artisan	exports	profits	total demand
traditional agriculture	$a_{11}X_1$	$a_{12}X_1$	$a_{13}X_1$	$a_{14}X_1$	$a_{15}X_1$	$a_{16}X_1$	$a_{17}X_1$	$a_{18}X_1$	$\sum_{i=1}^{8} a_{1i}X_1$
modern agriculture	$a_{21}X_2$	$a_{22}X_2$	$a_{23}X_2$	$a_{24}X_2$	$a_{25}X_2$	$a_{26}X_2$	$a_{27}X_2$	$a_{28}X_2$	$\sum_{i=1}^{8} a_{2i}X_2$
manufacturing	$a_{31}X_3$	$a_{32}X_3$	$a_{33}X_3$	$a_{34}X_3$	$a_{35}X_3$	$a_{36}X_3$	$a_{37}X_3$	$a_{38}X_3$	$\sum_{i=1}^{8} a_{3i}X_3$
proprietors	$a_{41}X_4$	$a_{42}X_4$	$a_{43}X_4$	$a_{44}X_4$	$a_{45}X_4$	$a_{46}X_4$	$a_{47}X_4$	$a_{48}X_4$	$\sum_{i=1}^{8} a_{4i}X_4$
farm income	$a_{51}X_5$	$a_{52}X_5$	$a_{53}X_5$	$a_{54}X_5$	$a_{55}X_5$	$a_{56}X_5$	$a_{57}X_5$	$a_{58}X_5$	$\sum_{i=1}^{8} a_{5i}X_5$
manufacturing income	$a_{61}X_6$	$a_{62}X_6$	$a_{63}X_6$	$a_{64}X_6$	$a_{65}X_6$	$a_{66}X_6$	$a_{67}X_6$	$a_{68}X_6$	$\sum_{i=1}^{8} a_{6i}X_6$
imports (manufacturing)	$a_{71}X_7$	$a_{72}X_7$	$a_{73}X_7$	$a_{74}X_7$	$a_{75}X_7$	$a_{76}X_7$	$a_{77}X_7$	$a_{78}X_7$	$\sum_{i=1}^{8} a_{7i}X_7$
capital accumulation	$a_{81}X_8$	$a_{82}X_8$	$a_{83}X_8$	$a_{84}X_8$	$a_{85}X_8$	$a_{86}X_8$	$a_{87}X_8$	$a_{88}X_8$	$\sum_{i=1}^{8} a_{8i}X_8$
total purchases	$\sum_{j=1}^{8} a_{i1}X_j$	$\sum_{j=1}^{8} a_{i2}X_j$	$\sum_{j=1}^{8} a_{i3}X_j$	$\sum_{j=1}^{8} a_{i4}X_j$	$\sum_{j=1}^{8} a_{i5}X_j$	$\sum_{j=1}^{8} a_{i6}X_j$	$\sum_{j=1}^{8} a_{i7}X_j$	$\sum_{j=1}^{8} a_{i8}X_j$	$\sum_{ij=1}^{8} a_{ji}X_j$

er's profit. Some of this profit may be spent on consumption (thus increasing farm incomes); the remainder will be accumulated in one of the agricultural sectors and used in producing agricultural goods during the following year.   When more capital is employed, agricultural output will increase again. This increase will take two forms.   First, more capital will be used in the agriculture sector where it has accumulated. Second, the accumulation of capital in the traditional agriculture sector will transform it. The additional capital will enable farmers using traditional agricultural methods to employ modern methods.   Our input-output table for the following year will show an increase in all inputs into modern agriculture and a decrease in all inputs into traditional agriculture. Inputs which now appear under the traditional sector column will appear in succeeding input-output tables under the modern agriculture heading. Since the surplus is greater per acre in modern agriculture, transformation from traditional to modern agriculture will again increase the surplus generated in the agricultural sectors. Again, with rents being fixed, profits accrue to farmers and more capital is accumulated, resulting in further growth.

What does all this tell us about Quesnay's *Tableau*?   What light does it shed on Quesnay's zig-zags and his growth model?

I think that the answer to these questions must be "very little."   We have already seen the reasons for such an evaluation. Certainly all the failures of static input-output reconstructions carry over to the dynamic reconstruction of Barna.   The problems with prior attempts at reconstructing the dynamic *Tableau* presented in Chapter IV likewise carry over to Barna's version of the dynamic *Tableau*.

Let us consider, as we did in Chapter IV, a change in spending propensities. Suppose we are in static equilibrium and all classes begin spending 3/5 of their income on manufactured goods. We saw in Chapter IV that this leaves the agricultural sector with additional food at the end of the circulation period. The agricultural sector has thus accumulated capital in the form of food or seed. According to Barna's analysis, there should then be a transition from traditional to modern agriculture.   But this is one of Quesnay's examples of economic decline.   Agricultural output should be reduced.

In contrast, the output of manufactured goods should increase (albeit temporarily). Barna, though, provides no mechanism for this result. Moreover, the manufacturing sector received neither

profits nor accumulates capital according to Barna's analysis.[151]
So $2000 of inputs in the manufacturing sector mysteriously are
transformed into $2211 manufactured goods with neither a surplus
nor profit.

Similar problems result when all classes increase spending on
agricultural goods.   To start the growth process for Barna, profits
must arise in the agricultural sector.   Profits require either an
increase in the agricultural surplus with prices fixed, or an increase
in the price of agricultural goods. The agricultural surplus, though,
will not increase until increased profits are deployed in modernizing
the agricultural sector. That only leaves a price increase as a possible
explanation for the emergence of profit in the agricultural sector.
However this possibility was shown to be impossible when discussing
Woog's reconstruction in Chapter IV.   Consequently, Barna's
proposal can explain neither the economic growth nor the economic
decline that results from changes in spending propensities.

Finally,   insofar   as   capital   accumulation   modernizes
agriculture, there is a shift from traditional to modern agriculture.
But how is this to be represented within input-output   analysis?
Leontief   maintained   that   structural   coefficients   must   be
constant.[152] If they are not, then any dynamic Leontief system of
equations will be underdetermined.   Reconsider the Leontief
equations representing a two sector economy over three years with
which we began this chapter. These six equations contained eight
unknowns. Only if output in one year were given could we reduce
the number of unknowns to six and solve the system. But if the
input-output coefficients, a_{ij}, are also variables of the system, then we
have twelve additional variables and no means of solving the system.
This is why Leontief had to stipulate that input-output coefficients be
constant.   But since it is part of Quesnay's system that these
parameters change—that is, since the mechanism by which the
economy   grows   and   declines   *is*   a   change   in   input-output
ratios—input-output analysis cannot be very helpful in explaining the
dynamic *Tableau*.

---

[151] Barna, "Quesnay's Model...," p. 321.

[152] According to Pasinetti, this is the major limitation of the Leontief system. He
argues that by assuming technical coefficients are constant, input-output analysis
becomes useless for analyzing dynamic economic systems, where technical change is
highly relevant. Luigi L. Pasinetti, *Lectures on the Theory of Production* (New York:
Columbia University Press, 1977), p. 69f.

CHAPTER VI
APPLICATIONS OF THE *TABLEAU*

Chapters III and IV examined the workings of the *Tableau*. In Chapter III the exchange and production relations of the static *Tableau* were explained. While Chapter IV explained the dynamic *Tableau*. In Chapter IV, changes in population and changes in agricultural sector productivity were shown to be the key mechanisms lying behind the dynamic *Tableau*.

In this chapter we shift our focus from the workings of the *Tableau* to its applications. One important application—the effects of the over- and under-consumption of agricultural goods—has already been examined. This result will be developed further in Section IV of this chapter, where Quesnay's analysis of misconsumption will be expanded into a theory of the business cycle that is quite different from the usual business cycle theories. But first we shall look at some other applications of the *Tableau*.

The early editions of the *Tableau* all assumed no savings. This assumption was relaxed by Quesnay in his later works. *Tableaux* were set forth in which money was hoarded and the economic decline resulting from such hoarding was demonstrated. These *Tableaux* will be examined in Section I. Section II concerns prices. Quesnay frequently remarked that a high price for agricultural goods was necessary for a prosperous economy. In his later works, he set forth several *Tableaux* designed to demonstrate how a high price for agricultural goods will result in economic growth. We will look at these *Tableaux* and Quesnay's explanation of the effect of high agricultural prices in Section II. Finally, one of the Physiocrat's more famous policy prescriptions was the doctrine of the single tax. Fiscal policy, the Physiocrats argued, should impose taxes only on the agricultural surplus. Taxes placed elsewhere would result in economic decline. Quesnay's argument and analysis on this point are examined in Section III.

We saw in Chapter II that the no savings assumption was included by Quesnay as part of all three editions of the *Tableau*.

135

Even before he developed the *Tableau,* Quesnay saw that unspent savings would result in economic decline. The early *Encyclopedia* articles all warn of the harmful effects of hoarding.

While Quesnay recognized that hoarding would lead to economic decline and that the static *Tableau* therefore required the assumption of no savings, nowhere in the *Encyclopedia* articles or in the three editions of the *Tableau* does he attempt to demonstrate these results. These works contain no *Tableaux* analyzing the effects of hoarding on the economy. Even in *L'Ami des Hommes,* where Quesnay describes in detail the effects of harding, he fails to demonstrate the effects of hoarding by means of a series of *Tableaux.*[153] The analysis below is therefore a formalization and elucidation of Quesnay's analysis.

Let us begin the analysis by examining the effects of hoarding by the two producing classes. We assume each producing class saves 10% of its money receipts; the remaining 90% is spent— half on agricultural goods and half on manufactured goods. Also it is necessary to assume that none of the money saved gets invested, or used as a means of production in the future. Finally, we assume that the reduced spending on agricultural goods does not reduce productivity in the agricultural sector. These assumptions about spending, saving, and reproduction cause output to decline. Production declines because with the lack of demand for its output, each producing sector fails to obtain the needed inputs for future production. Figure #6-1, which adds two columns showing sectoral hoarding to the traditional zig-zag presentation of the *Tableau,* depicts economic decline in the next production period as a result of current savings by the two producing classes.

The reduction in output as a result of hoarding will be a function of the propensity to hoard. In general, where

h' = the propensity to hoard by each producing class

h = $1-h'$ = the propensity to spend by each producing class

a = the propensity to consume agricultural goods by all classes

b = the propensity to consume manufactured goods by all classes

---

[153] Mirabeau and Quesnay, *L'Ami des Hommes* (Avignon, 1762), Vol 5, Part VI, pp. 92-101.

and R = proprietor rents

hoarding by each producing class will equal h´ times the income received by that class. From our assumption•that all spending is divided equally between agricultural goods and manufactured goods, it follows that each producing sector receives aR (= bR) from the proprietors and hoards h´aR (= h´bR). From the other producing sector a sequence of incomes is received:

$$Rahb + Rah^2b^2 + Ra^2h^3b^2 + Ra^2h^4b^3 + ...$$

FIGURE #6-1

THE *TABLEAU* WITH 10% SAVED BY THE TWO PRODUCING CLASSES

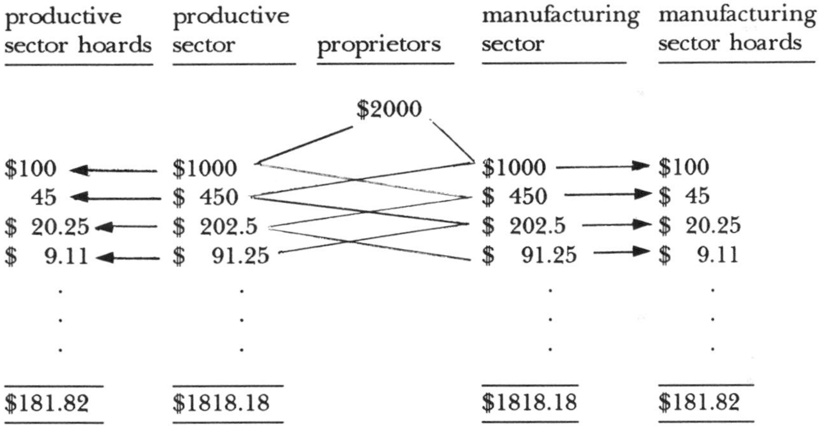

productive sector hoards	productive sector	proprietors	manufacturing sector	manufacturing sector hoards
		$2000		
$100	$1000		$1000	$100
45	$ 450		$ 450	$ 45
$ 20.25	$ 202.5		$ 202.5	$ 20.25
$ 9.11	$ 91.25		$ 91.25	$ 9.11
.	.		.	.
.	.		.	.
.	.		.	.
$181.82	$1818.18		$1818.18	$181.82

This sequence sums to:

$$R \left[\frac{ahb + a^2h^2b}{1 - h^2 \, ba} \right]$$

When a=b=.5 and R = \$2000, manufacturing and agricultural receipts from one another are each \$818.18. From this, 10% or \$81.82 is saved. Added to the receipts and hoards resulting from proprietor spending, the agricultural and manufacturing classes each receive \$1818.18 and each hoard \$181.82. These are the figures which appear as column totals in Figure #6-1.

In general, hoards of the manufacturing sector will be equal

to $h'bR + hR \left[\dfrac{ahb + a^2h^2b}{1-h^2\,ba}\right]$ and hoards of the agricultural sector

will be equal to $h'\,aR + h'\,R\left[\dfrac{ahb + ah^2b^2}{1-h^2\,ba}\right]$.

Manufacturing receipts will be:

$$bR + R\left[\frac{ahb + a^2h^2b}{1-h^2ba}\right] - bR\left[1+\frac{ah + a^2h^2}{1-h^2ba}\right] \qquad (1)$$

and agricultural sector receipts will be:

$$aR + R\left[\frac{ahb + ah^2b^2}{1-h^2\,ba}\right] - aR\left[1 + \frac{bh + b^2h^2}{1 - h^2ba}\right] \qquad (2)$$

When h=1, there is no saving. Manufacturing receipts reduce to:

$bR\left[1 + \dfrac{a + a^2}{1-ba}\right]$, while agricultural sector receipts reduce to:

$aR\left[1 + \dfrac{b + b^2}{1-ba}\right]$. When, in addition, a=b=.5 both fractions

inside the brackets equal 1, and we have a *Tableau* in static equilibrium. Receipts of each producing class equal R, proprietor rents. This is the solution to the static *Tableau*.

As h, the propensity to spend falls, agricultural and manufacturing sector receipts drop. The numerators of the fractions within the brackets of equations (1) and (2) fall, and the denominators rises. Agricultural and manufacturing sector output falls, and the economy declines. As h approaches 0, the fractions in the brackets of equations (1) and (2) approach 0. Manufacturing receipts approach bR and agricultural receipts approach aR. The two producing classes receive only what the proprietors spend.

We shall now introduce hoarding by the proprietors. Figure #6-2 below is a *Tableau* demonstrating the effects of proprietors saving 10% of their rent receipts. For the moment it is assumed that there is no hoarding by the producing classes. Proprietor hoards are shown under their column. We start again from an economy in static equilibrium with the net product equal to $2000. As Figure #6-2 shows, proprietor hoarding of $200 reduces expenditure on agricultural and manufactured goods by $200 apiece. In general

FIGURE #6-2

THE *TABLEAU* WITH 10% SAVED BY THE PROPRIETORS

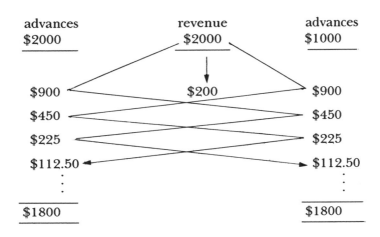

where
k' = the proprietors' propensity to save, and
$k = 1-k'$ = the proprietors' propensity to spend,
the agricultural sector receives akR from the proprietors. The agricultural class also receives a stream of income from the manufacturing sector. This will be similar to the stream we derived in Chapter IV. The major difference is that now the effective demand of the proprietors—kR—rather than proprietor rents is the important variable. Agricultural sector receipts due to manufacturing class expenditures will equal $abkR + a^2bkR + a^2b^2kR + ...$, which

sums to $\dfrac{abkR + a^2bkR}{1-ab}$. Total agricultural

sector receipts are then

$$akR + \frac{abkR + a^2bkR}{1-ab}. \tag{3}$$

Manufacturing sector receipts will differ only in that the a's and b's of equation (3) will be switched.   From the proprietors the manufacturing class receives bkR, and from the agricultural class it receives $\dfrac{abkR + b^2akR}{1-ab}$. Total manufacturing receipts are

thus

$$bkR + \frac{abkR + b^2akR}{1-ab}. \tag{4}$$

When a=b=.5 and k=.1, agricultural sector receipts are \$1800 and manufacturing sector receipts are \$1800.   Minor algebraic manipulation gives us the following expression for agricultural receipts

$$kR \left[\frac{b - b^2 a + ab + a^2 b}{1-ab} \right] \tag{5}$$

while manufacturing sector receipts are equal to:

$$kR \left[\frac{b - b^2 a + ab + a^2 b}{1-ab} \right]. \tag{6}$$

When all classes consume equal amounts of agricultural and manufactured goods, equations (5) and (6) each reduce to

$$kR \left[\frac{a + ab}{1-ab} \right].$$

When k=1, there is no hoarding and we have equilibrium in a static *Tableau*. As k falls, hoarding increases and the receipts of both producing sectors decline. They decline by the percentage k, and will continue to do so until k increases to 1 and hoarding ends. This is because when agricultural receipts decline, agricultural output declines by twice this amount. The agricultural surplus and hence proprietor revenues decline in succeeding periods. As long as a fraction of this lower revenue is hoarded, economic decline will continue.

Finally, we can examine the effects of hoarding by the proprietors and by the two producing classes. With hoarding by all classes, agricultural sector receipts will be

$$kaR \left[1 + \frac{bh + b^2h^2}{1 - h^2ba} \right] \tag{7}$$

and manufacturing sector receipts will be

$$kbR \left[1 + \frac{ah + a^2h^2}{1 - h^2ba} \right]. \tag{8}$$

Hoarding means that k or h is less than 1. When this happens both agricultural and manufacturing sector output declines. In addition, the slack demand for agricultural goods reduces both the output of agricultural goods and the agricultural surplus in succeeding periods. This causes a fall in R resulting in further declines in output. To prevent continual declines in output the revenues of the proprietors, R, must be kept from falling. Only if the propensity to consume agricultural goods increases to offset the fall in demand for agricultural goods due to saving will agricultural sector receipts remain constant. The condition which must be met in order that the economy not continually decline will be:

$$kaR \left[1 + \frac{bh + b^2h^2}{1 - h^2ba} \right] - R \tag{9}$$

which can be manipulated to:

$$a - k + \frac{kbh + b^2h^2k}{1-h^2ba}. \qquad (10)$$

Since b + a = 1,

$$a - k + \frac{kbh + b^2h^2k}{1-h^2b(1-b)}. \qquad (11)$$

As hoarding increases, k and h increase. To prevent dynamic decline the propensity to consume agricultural goods, a, must increase to offset the hoarding. When the consumption of agricultural goods increases to exactly offset the reduced demand for agricultural goods due to hoarding, there is no decline in agricultural output and no decline in proprietor rents. This occurs if and only if the condition of equation (11) is met. Manufacturing output, however, must be lower than before we introduced hoarding. It will decline because of the change in spending propensities, which now favors agricultural goods, and because of the hoarding. But this is a once and for all decline. It does not lead to further declines as long as proprietor rents remain constant. For it is the new effective demand generated by changed proprietor incomes that introduces the dynamic aspect to the *Tableau*.

SECTION II

In August 1977 Quesnay's article "Probleme Economique" appeared in the *Journal de 'l Agriculture du Commerce et des Finances*. Because of another article with the same title, this work has come to be known as "The First Economic Problem." The other article, dealing with the effects of taxation, has come to be known as "The Second Economic Problem." This later article will be dealt with in the next section.

"The First Economic Problem" was written to demonstrate a proposition Quesnay had maintained for a number of years—high prices for agricultural goods are extremely desirable. As early as his *Encyclopedia* article "Corn," Quesnay noted the harmful effects of a low price for corn. Workers became lazy; farmers had difficulty finding workers; and servants served badly.[154] In contrast, a high price compensates the cultivator for his costs and prevents the agricultural sector from declining.[155] An identical position is held in all three editions of the *Tableau*.[156]

Quesnay's early view was that the price of corn or produce must remain high. This view is expressed in "Corn" and in the various editions of the *Tableau*. "The First Economic Problem" contains the assumption that high prices in general are desirable. Quesnay's example in this work has the price of both agricultural and manufactured goods increase. There is really no inconsistency in these positions, just a difference of emphasis. Quesnay thought that the price of manufactured goods is determined by their costs of production. Moreover, as we have seen, the manufacturing sector obtains almost all of its inputs from the agricultural sector. Thus, when it costs the manufacturing class more to obtain food and raw materials, the price of manufactured goods must increase.

In *Philosophie Rurale* Quesnay employs the *Tableau* for the first time to show the economic effects of a change in price. We have previously examined this *Tableau* in Chapter II. A more detailed *Tableau* and a description of the effects of price changes is contained in "The First Economic Problem." Here Quesnay begins with a static *Tableau* in equilibrium, constructed on the assumption of low and stable prices. He then assumes a change in economic policy. Free trade, both foreign and domestic, become the new policies of the French government. Their implementation results in high and stable prices for all goods. Quesnay also identified other policies as having the same effect. Encouragement of trade; abolition of privileges, prohibitions, and taxes; and increased communications would all tend to stabilize prices at a high level.[157]

Quesnay's analysis of the economic impact of high prices in "The First Economic Problem" is quite complex, as he is the first to admit.[158] His argument can be set forth more clearly by making a number of simplifying assumptions. Indirect taxes, interest goods,

---

[154] Meek, *Economics of Physiocracy*, p. 86.

[155] Ibid., p. 76.

[156] See Remarks #12 and #13 of the first edition of the *Tableau* and Maxims #12 and #13 of the second and third edition.

[157] See Henry Woog, *The Tableau Économique of François Quesnay* (Bern: A. Francke A. G. Verlag, 1950), p. 90 and the references cited therein.

[158] Meek, *Economics of Physiocracy*, p. 168.

and the governmental sector all can be ignored, as we have previously done. And rather than considering the effects of a price increase by one-sixth, which leads to messy computations, we consider the effects of prices doubling.

In addition to needless complications, several errors on Quesnay's part confuse matters further.   Any analysis of the consequences of a price change must distinguish real from nominal variables.   This is not done in "The First Economic Problem." Quesnay begins by arguing that an increase in prices will increase the value of agricultural output by more than it increases the value of agricultural inputs. Hence surplus value must rise. While it is true that for any given surplus, an increase in price will raise the value of that surplus, this does *not* mean that real output, or the surplus itself, increases. When prices rise there may still be the same quantity of commodities produced. In this case, the price increase is not equivalent to an increase in output. Unless real and nominal effects are distinguished we cannot say whether the quantity of commodities produced has increased, or just their price.

Quesnay's confusion on this point also surfaces when he discusses the effect of price increases on the profits of the cultivator. He contends that higher prices will increase the profits of the cultivator by one-tenth "without causing any damage to the purchaser-consumer."[159] There are only two ways this could be so, and so only two things Quesnay might mean here. These two possibilities correspond to the two possible interpretations of profit. Cultivators in the agricultural sector could find that *real profits have increased* due to the price increase, or it may be that *nominal profits increase with real profits unaffected*. If Quesnay's position here is that profits have increased in real terms he has begged the question he was supposed to prove.   When prices of agricultural and manufactured goods increase by the same proportion, the only way real profits in the agricultural sector can rise is for productivity in the agricultural sector to rise. In this case real agricultural output will increase.   Why agricultural productivity should increase is left unexplained however. On the other hand, Quesnay's position might be that profits increase only in nominal terms, with all real variables remaining unaffected. In this case the benefit to the economy of a price rise is not clear. Prices go up, but real output is unchanged.

---

[159] Ibid., p. 172.

Finally, the confusion between real and nominal variables is compounded by the *Tableau* Quesnay provides in order to demonstrate the economic effects of a price change. Figure #6-3 reproduces the *Tableau* from "The First Economic Problem."[160]

figure #6-3
TABLEAU FROM "THE FIRST ECONOMIC PROBLEM"

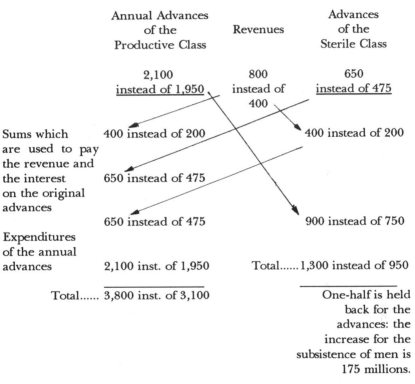

Annual Advances of the Productive Class	Revenues	Advances of the Sterile Class
2,100 instead of 1,950	800 instead of 400	650 instead of 475

Sums which are used to pay the revenue and the interest on the original advances

400 instead of 200   400 instead of 200

650 instead of 475

Expenditures of the annual advances

650 instead of 475   900 instead of 750

2,100 inst. of 1,950   Total...... 1,300 instead of 950

Total...... 3,800 inst. of 3,100

One-half is held back for the advances: the increase for the subsistence of men is 175 millions.

This *Tableau* contains figures for revenues, advances, expenditures, and output both before and after a price change. Agricultural advances are initially $1950. These advances are $750 of manufactured goods, $750 of agricultural goods, and $450 to be paid as indirect taxes. Only manufactured goods will increase in price because only these commodities are obtained by the agricultural class via trade. If these manufactured goods increase in

---

price by one-sixth, their cost will rise by $125 to $875. Quesnay rounds this off to $900, thus making advances in agriculture now $2100.

Proprietor revenues increase from $400 to $800 due to two factors. First, the value of the agricultural surplus increases. Since advances are $1950 initially, the agricultural surplus must be $1950 initially. Increasing by one-sixth, the surplus increases in value by $325, which Quesnay rounds off to $320. Inexplicably, Quesnay subtracts a $150 increase in input costs, making the net increase $170. Since changes in input costs are already taken into account when deriving the value of the net product this adjustment by Quesnay is unnessary. A second source of increase in proprietor revenues comes from a 10% increase in profits for the cultivator. This is calculated by Quesnay to be $235, based on sales of $2350 by the agricultural sector. Since we have already accounted for nominal increases in profits and the net product, the increase in profits here can only mean an increase in real profits. However, Quesnay provides no explanation for the increase. Nor does he explain how the $2350 figure was arrived at. This figure appears nowhere in the *Tableau* and is not the sum of any figures contained in Figure #6-3.

Finally, manufacturing sector advances increase from $475 to $650. Once again, Quesnay provides neither justification nor explanation for this increase.

In addition to these dubious changes in advances and revenues, there are several serious problems with the distribution process of Figure #6-3. We have seen previously that neither producing class has advances in the form of money. Yet, in Figure #6-3 both producing classes spend their advances on the output of the other producing sector. The agricultural class spends $900 of its advances on manufactured goods, and the sterile class spends its entire advances—$650—on agricultural goods. Productive sector advances are also spent twice. The productive spends $900 of its advances on manufactured goods, and also spends all its advances within the agricultural sector. This is the $2100 denoted "expenditure of annual advances" under the productive class column.

The distribution process is also confused because the analysis is couched in nominal terms, and it is not clear what is happening in real terms. Finally, Figure #6-3 suffers, as do all Quesnay's presentations of the *Tableau*, because it does not show what is happening to money during the production and distribution process. We are never certain that a class has the money to make the purchase required of it at a particular time. Nor does Quesnay say anything about where the productive sector obtains the additional money it needs to pay the proprietors twice as much in rent.

These problems can be illustrated using the following much simpler example, which considers the effects of a doubling in price. We begin with our tabular reconstruction right before the production of agricultural or manufacturing goods takes place, and we begin with by assuming that a unit of each commodity sells for $1. Before prices change, class holdings and their values will be:

Productive Class	*Proprietors*	*Manufacturing Class*
$2000 money	$1000 food (1000	$1000 raw materials
$1000 food (1000	units)	(1000 units)
units)	$1000 mfg'd goods	$ 500 mfg'd goods
$1000 mfg'd goods	(1000 units)	(500 units)
(1000 units)		$ 500 food (500
		units)

The doubling of prices changes the value of class holdings; quantities, of course, are left unchanged.

Productive Class	*Proprietors*	*Manufacturing Class*
$2000 money	$2000 food (1000	$2000 raw materials
$1000 food (1000	units	(1000 units)
units)	$2000 mfg'd goods	$1000 mfg'd goods
$2000 mfg'd goods	(1000 units)	(500 units)
(1000 units)		$1000 food (500
		units)

It should be noted that the value of food within the productive sector has not changed. This is in accord with Quesnay's contention that only goods bought and sold on the intersectoral market change in price. The corn used by the farmer for food and for seed does not involve such exchange, and so does not change in price.

Production and consumption now take place. Input-output assumptions are as usual, but it is quantities that are crucial rather than prices. The productive sector employs 1000 units of food and 1000 units of manufactured goods in producing 3000 units of food and 1000 units of raw materials. The value of the inputs employed in the agricultural sector was $3000. The value of agricultural output will now be $7000. The 1000 units of raw materials will be sold to the manufacturing class for $2000. 1000 units of food will be sold to the proprietors and 1000 units will be sold to the manufacturing class; the third 1000 units will be held for consumption by the cultivators. Thus the value of food sold to other classes is $4000, and the value of food maintained for internal consumption will be $1000. Added to the value of raw materials, this makes the total value of agricultural output $7000, and the surplus value created in agriculture is $4000. This will be the proprietors' rent in the next period. The increase in surplus value is not affected by Quensay's assumption that food inputs used in agriculture do not change in price. Were they to do so, the value of both inputs and outputs would increase by $1000 leaving surplus value at $4000.

In the manufacturing sector, 2000 units of manufactured goods will be produced. Since the entire output of manufactured goods is sold to other classes, the value of this output of manufactured goods is sold to other classes, the value of this output (when prices have doubled) will be $4000. Following production class holdings thus become:

Productive Class	*Proprietors*	*Manufacturing Class*
$1000 food (1000 units)	($4000 in rent claims)	$4000 mfg'd goods (2000 units)
$4000 food (2000 units)		
$2000 raw materials (1000 units)		
$2000 money		

At this point a problem with the *Tableau* of the "The First Economic Problem" arises. The productive class owes $4000 to the proprietors. Yet it has only $2000 of money with which to pay rents. To obtain additional money, some commodities must be sold abroad. Let us suppose cultivators export their 1000 units of food. This food will sell for $2000, given the recent price rise. It will provide the productive class with sufficient money to pay the proprietors. These two transactions yield:

Productive Class	*Proprietors*	*Manufacturing Class*
$4000 food (2000 units)	$4000 money	$4000 mfg'd goods (2000 units)
$2000 raw materials (1000 units)		

Circulation can now follow the usual pattern. The proprietors will buy $2000 food and $2000 manufactured goods; the manufacturing class will buy $2000 food; the productive class will buy $2000 manufactured goods; and the manufacturing class will buy $2000 of raw materials, then export $1000 food and import $1000 manufactured goods. Following these transactions production should take place in both the agricultural and manufacturing sectors. But as the table below shows, the productive class lacks food.

Productive Class	Proprietors	Manufacturing Class
$4000 money	$2000 food (1000	$2000 raw materials
$2000 mfg'd goods	units)	(1000 units)
(1000 units)	$2000 mfg'd goods	$1000 food (500 units
	(1000 units)	$1000 mfg'd goods
		(500 units)

To simplify things let us assume the productive class imports 1000 units of food. This reduces their stock of money to $2000 and, in essence, returns the food originally exported. Production can now take place and reproduction can continue year after year following this sequence.

Here we run into the major problem with Quesnay's argument. Although the value of rents and the value of output have increased, in real terms there has been no change. The productive class continues to produce 4000 units of agricultural goods, the manufacturing class continues to produce 2000 units of manufactured goods, and the proprietors continue to consume the surplus in the form of 1000 units of food and 1000 units of manufactured goods. Quesnay's argument that a price increase leads to economic growth is wrong. Quesnay goes wrong because he fails to distinguish real from nominal effects of a price change. All figures in the *Tableau* are prices, so an increase in these numbers means little. To demonstrate the effect of a price rise on the real economy Quesnay would have to distinguish real from nominal effects of the change, and argue that real output, as well as nominal output, increases with prices.

Towards this end, at the very end of "The First Economic Problem" Quesnay introduces the assumption that rents are sticky upward.

> The farmers of landed property profit up to the renewal
> of their leases from the constant increase in the prices of
> products which occurs during the terms of these leases.

And this gain is most fruitful, most profitable, and most necessary in a nation whose agriculture is in need of extension and improvement. For . . . the profits which they make increase the wealth which they employ in cultivation, which is greatly to the advantage of agriculture.[161]

According to Quesnay, rents are fixed in contracts of several years. Contractual rent payments will be the average agricultural surplus over the past several years. Increases in surplus value due to price changes will *not immediately go to the proprietors* as higher rents. Only when rental contracts are renegotiated will competition among the cultivators cause the rents to reflect the greater surplus value. A similar principle is contained in *Philosophie Rurale*.[162] There it is assumed that for any change in agricultural output, half will be borne by the cultivators of the land. The cultivators will then experience an increase or decrease in advances that is equal to half the change in agricultural output.

This view contrasts with the *Tableau* we have just examined and with Quesnay's example in "The First Economic problem." The major difference is that now price increases raise the incomes of the cultivators of the land at the expense of the proprietors, whose rents are fixed. As such, the cultivators will now be able to afford more advanced agricultural techniques. Employing better technology, agricultural productivity, and hence the real surplus, will rise.

The following sequence of tables illustrates this point. It is again assumed that all prices double from $1 per unit to $2 per unit. This time though we assume that rents are unchanged when prices increase. These assumptions give us the following holdings when prices rise:

Productive Class	Proprietors	Manufacturing Class
$2000 food (1000 units)	$2000 food (1000 units)	$2000 raw materials (1000 units)
$2000 mfg'd goods (1000 units)	$2000 mfg'd goods (1000 units)	$1000 food (500 units)
		$1000 mfg'd goods (500 units)

---

[161] Ibid., p. 180.

[162] François Quesnay, *Philosophie Rurale* (Amsterdam: Chez Les Libraires Associes, 1764), Vol. III, pp. 33-53.

We make the same input-output assumptions as before. Now, however, rents remain fixed at $2000, so the cultivators do not need to sell some food abroad in order to obtain additional money. As we will see, after production and distribution take place the productive class will have an extra 500 units of food. This will result from the reduced purchasing power of the proprietors. Following production and rent payments, class holdings will be:

Productive Class	*Proprietors*	*Manufacturing Class*
$6000 food (3000 units)	$2000 money	$4000 mfg'd goods (2000 units)
$2000 raw materials (1000 units)		

The distribution process begins with proprietors spending their rents. As usual, half is spent on manufactured goods and half on food. This gives us:

Productive Class	*Proprietors*	*Manufacturing Class*
$5000 food (2500 units)	$1000 food (500 units)	$3000 mfg'd goods (1500 units)
$2000 raw materials (1000 units)	$1000 mfg'd goods (500 units)	$1000 money
$1000 money		

In accord with the Tableau's zig-zags, the manufacturing class buys $1000 food and the productive class buys $1000 manufactured goods. Holdings become:

Productive Class	*Proprietors*	*Manufacturing Class*
$4000 food (2000 units)	$1000 food (500 units)	$2000 mfg'd goods (1000 units)
$2000 raw materials (1000 units)	$1000 mfg'd goods (500 units)	$1000 food (500 units)
$1000 mfg'd goods (500 units)		$1000 money
$1000 money		

The manufacturing class now buys raw materials, resulting in:

Productive Class	*Proprietors*	*Manufacturing Class*
$4000 food (2000 units)	$1000 food (500 units)	$2000 mfg'd goods (1000 units)

$1000 raw materials $1000 mfg'd goods $1000 food
  (500 units)   (500 units)   (500 units)
$1000 mfg'd goods $1000 raw materials
  (500 units)   (500 units)
$2000 money

At this point the manufacturing class needs additional raw materials if it is to produce $4000 worth of manufactured goods. Employing the usual input-output assumption, $2000 (1000 units) of raw materials are necessary. On the other hand, the agricultural class needs additional manufactured goods if it is to produce $7000 food. If the economy is to reproduce itself, a new step needs to be introduced into the circulation process. Analytically, this new step represents an increase in velocity. In terms of the zig-zags, each producing class now spends a greater fraction of its money receipts on the commodities of the other producing class. Trade between the two producing classes, or the velocity of money, rises.

It is likely Quesnay saw that this was necessary. His *Tableau* showing the effects of a price change on the economy—Figure #6-3—contains an increase in the velocity of money. According to this diagram, the productive and sterile classes each receive $400 from the spending of the proprietors. On the old assumption that each producing class spends half its receipts on the goods of the other producing class, the agricultural class would spend $400 on manufactured goods and the sterile class would spend $400 on agricultural goods. But Figure #6-3 shows the sterile class spending $650 on agricultural goods and the agricultural class spending $900 on manufactured goods. This is possible if and only if trade, or the velocity of money, increases. We can account for this in our series of Meekian tables by an additional transaction. This will represent the increased intersectoral trade. We assume the productive class spends another $2000 on manufactured goods, and that the sterile class spends $2000 on agricultural goods. To simplify, it will be assumed that the manufacturing sector buys $1000 raw materials and $1000 food. These transactions give us:

Productive Class   *Proprietors*   *Manufacturing Class*
$3000 food $1000 food $2000 food
  (1500 units)   (500 units)   (1000 units)
$3000 mfg'd goods $1000 mfg'd goods $1000 raw materials
  (1500 units)   (500 units)   (500 units)
$2000 money

We are now ready for foreign trade to take place. The manufacturing class exports $1000 (500 units) of food, and imports $1000 (500 units) of manufactured goods. It is assumed by Quesnay that domestic and international prices are the same.[163] Following foreign trade we have:

Productive Class	Proprietors	Manufacturing Class
$3000 food (1500 (500 units)	$1000 food (500 units)	$1000 food (500 units)
$3000 mfg'd goods (1500 units)	$1000 mfg'd goods (500 units)	$2000 raw materials
$2000 money		$1000 mfg'd goods (500 units)

Production and consumption can now take place in accord with the usual input-output assumptions. The manufacturing sector produces 2000 units of manufactured goods, whose value will be $4000. In the agricultural sector, 1500 units of manufactured goods and 1500 units of food are used to produced 6000 units of agricultural goods. The value of agricultural inputs is $6000. The value of food and raw materials produced will be $12,000, and surplus value will be $6000. With rent payments fixed, the additional surplus is not expropriated by the proprietors, and can be used by the cultivators to employ better methods of cultivation, thus increasing agricultural productivity. Production and consumption bring us to the following position:

Productive Class	Proprietors	Manufacturing Class
$2000 raw materials (1000 units)	($2000 in rent claims)	$4000 mfg'd goods (2000 units)
$2000 money		
$10,000 food (5000 units)		

With rents fixed, a price increase leads to a reduction in the proprietors' real consumption. They consume 500 units apiece of food and manufactured goods rather than 1000 units. This leaves a larger portion of the economic pie for the two producing classes. The manufacturing class fails to benefit because the gains they get when the price of manufactured goods goes up is offset exactly by the

---

[163] Meek, *Economics of Physiocracy*, p. 93, 95, and *passim*.

increased price of agricultural inputs. Hence, all the benefits of the price increase go to the productive sector. This in turn will benefit the whole economy. Annual advances in agriculture can be increased, resulting in increased production in the future. The additional output of agricultural goods can also go to increasing original advances in the productive sector. This will increase productivity in agriculture. In both cases, the original increase in price leads to an increase in agricultural output in real terms.

SECTION III

The Physiocratic doctrine of taxation was originally developed in Quesnay's *Encyclopedia* articles. The theme running through these articles is that taxes ought not be laid on the cultivator. "If the sovereign imposes taxes on the cultivator. . . there is a decline in cultivation and a diminution in the proprietor's revenue, whence follows an inevitable retrenchment which affects hired people, merchants, workers and servants. The general system of expenditure, work, gain and consumption is thrown out of gear; the state grows weaker; and the tax comes to have a more and more destructive effect."[164]   Instead, Quesnay argues, taxes should be placed on the proprietor's revenue. This is the true wealth of the nation, and the only income that can be taxed without causing the economy to decline. All three editions of the *Tableau* contain maxims making a similar point—to obtain the high level of economic activity depicted in the diagrams, taxes must be laid directly on the proprietors.[165]

These remarks, however, were mere assertions. In neither the *Encyclopedia* articles nor the three editions of the *Tableau* does Quesnay demonstrate the harm resulting from a tax on the cultivators. Nor does he show there would be no decline if taxes were placed on proprietor revenues. Proof of these important Physiocratic doctrines was left to "The Second Economic Problem," which was first published in *Physiocratie*. In attempting to demonstrate the effects of taxation Quesnay employs three *Tableaux*. In the first, he sets forth a static *Tableau*, showing reproduction before the imposition of any tax. Next there is a *Tableau* showing

---

[164] Ibid., p. 82.
[165] This is usually Maxim #7. See Meek, *Economics of Physiocracy,* pp. 112, 121, and Kuczynski and Meek, *Quesnay's Tableau Économique,* p. 4f.

the effects of a tax placed on the revenue of the proprietors. Finally, the effects of an indirect tax on the cultivators is analyzed using a third *Tableau*. Comparison of the three *Tableaux* shows that a direct tax on the proprietors has only redistributional effects. There is no effect on production or output. In contrast, an indirect tax on the productive class reduces output from the figures presented in the original, static *Tableau*.

The three *Tableaux* Quesnay employs embody different assumptions than usual. In addition, Quesnay's example of the costs of indirect taxation involves the double and sometimes triple counting of losses, as well as several numerical errors. Even the specific losses themselves are rather difficult to comprehend. These flaws prompted Meek to write: "Quesnay's enthusiasm to prove his point seems to be running away with his logic here."[166] In this section we will see the extent to which this is true. But first, a look at Quesnay's argument.

Quesnay begins with a *Tableau* in static equilibrium, and with a base of $3000. Two new substantive assumptions are introduced. Usually Quesnay assumes that advances reproduce 100% in agriculture. But in "The Second Economic Problem," advances reproduce 200%. The second major change in Quesnay's assumptions concerns consumption. The static *Tableau* assumes all classes consume half their incomes as food and half as manufactured goods. In "The Second Economic Problem," however, the producing classes spend less than half their receipts on the goods of the other producing class. These two changes are obvious from an examination of Figure #6-4.[167]

The proprietors continue to spend half their income on agricultural goods and half their income on manufactured goods. If the two producing classes were to follow suit, they would purchase $1500 worth of goods from each other. However, the productive class purchases only $1000 of manufactured goods, while the manufacturing class purchases only $1250 of food. Spending propensities for the producing classes have thus changed. Figure #6-4 also makes clear that advances in agriculture ($2000) now result in the production of $6000 worth of agricultural goods. This is a 200% change.

---

[166] See the footnote on p. 199 of Meek, *Economics of Physiocracy*.
[167] Ibid.

FIGURE #6-4

THE STATIC *TABLEAU* FROM "THE SECOND ECONOMIC PROBLEM"

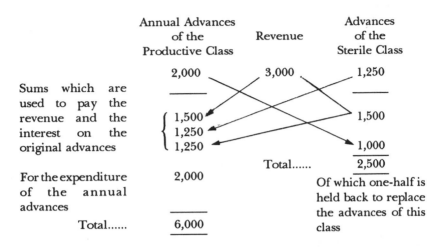

	Annual Advances of the Productive Class	Revenue	Advances of the Sterile Class
	2,000	3,000	1,250
Sums which are used to pay the revenue and the interest on the original advances	1,500 1,250 1,250		1,500 1,000
		Total......	2,500
For the expenditure of the annual advances	2,000		Of which one-half is held back to replace the advances of this class
Total......	6,000		

Rather than couching our analysis in terms of this *Tableau* with a new set of spending and input-output assumptions, we will return to the model of Chapter III, and follow Quesnay's analysis using the *Tableau* reconstructed there. This seems justified since we have already spent a considerable amount of time understanding how that *Tableau* works. Moreover, if the consequences of an indirect tax on the productive class are as Quesnay says, it should be possible to demonstrate these effects beginning with *any* static *Tableau*. Using the assumptions of the static *Tableau* from Chapter III is thus also a test of the generality of Quesnay's analysis.

We consider now the imposition of a direct tax on the proprietors. Quesnay opts for a tax of 2/7, or $800. This revenue, he claims, "would be sufficient on its own to maintain in the highest degree the magnificence and power of the sovereign authority and the expenditure necessary for the security and prosperity of the nation, but would not bring about any decline in the annual reproduction."[168]

It is relatively easy to show the effects of a direct tax on the proprietors with a zig-zag *Tableau*. This is done in Figure #6-5.

---

[168] Ibid., p. 189.   To simplify the analysis here, interest goods have been eliminated.

FIGURE #6-5

THE EFFECT OF A DIRECT TAX ON THE PROPRIETORS

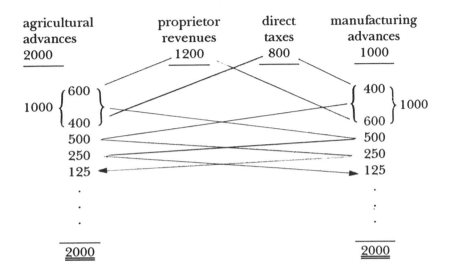

There are now two sets of zig-zags—one beginning with the proprietors, the other starting with the sovereign. The proprietors begin a stream of expenditures by purchasing $600 of food and $600 of manufactured goods. Similarly, the sovereign begins a stream of expenditures by purchasing $400 manufactured goods and $400 food. Proprietor and sovereign spending generate incomes for, and hence spending by, the two producing classes. From the proprietors and from the state each producing class receives $1000. This is spent, as usual, half on food and half on manufactured goods. Spending yields incomes, which in turn generates additional spending. The zig-zags work their way through the *Tableau* as always. Reproduction is nearly identical to reproduction before the imposition of the tax. The only difference is that the per capita consumption of the proprietors has been reduced to make way for consumption by the sovereign. A direct tax on the proprietor does not lead to any decline in the annual reproduction.

Quesnay recognized though that because of their "ignorant greed" the $800 tax is likely to "seem excessive to the landed proprietors."[169] They believe that direct taxes should only be 10% of their revenues, or $300; and they demand limitless exemptions and immunities form taxation. Opposition by the proprietors is so great that the sovereign must employ indirect taxes to obtain essential funds. A $300 direct tax on the proprietors would have no effect on reproduction, as the above analysis has shown. Employing indirect taxes though has disastrous consequences. Quesnay's third *Tableau* attempts to demonstrate this result.   To raise the $500 which the proprietors are unwilling to contribute, the sovereign must put into effect an indirect tax on consumption. A 9% sales tax will be necessary, since $5500 will be subject to the tax:

proprietor spending (less $300 in direct taxes)	$ 1700
state spending of direct taxes	300
productive class spending on manufacturers	1000
sterile expenditures on agricultural goods	2000
state spending of indirect tax receipts	500
	$ 5500

A tax of 9% on agricultural expenditures of $1000 generates $91 in revenue for the state.   However, it also reduces agricultural advances by $91. This reduces inputs necessary for reproduction. Since inputs reproduce 100%, a $91 reduction in inputs means $182 fewer agricultural goods are produced. *Gross* output falls $182, and the net product has declined $91. In addition, Quesnay maintains that the advances of the cultivators cannot be allowed to fall permanently as a result of taxation.   For this would destroy all advances in a few years. Agricultural advances must remain $2000. This is possible only if the proprietors are paid $91 less than the net product. The total decrease in proprietor rents is then $182—the reduction in the net product, plus the $91 used to maintain agricultural advances at $2000.   Reduced revenues for the proprietors in turn reduces demand for both agricultural and manufactured goods. A new equilibrium comes to be established in which both agricultural and manufactured output have fallen. This decline is demonstrated in Quesnay's third *Tableau* from "The Second Economic Problem," which appears, slightly modified, as

---

[169] Ibid., p. 190.

Figure #6-6.[170]

FIGURE #6-6
THE EFFECT OF AN INDIRECT TAX

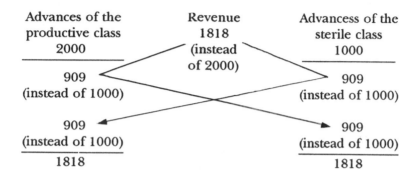

This is the essence of Quesnay's argument in "The Second Economic Problem." The argument, however, contains a very serious gap. What happens to the money collected by the sovereign? This money fails to appear in Figure #6-6. None of the tax monies collected is spent by the sovereign. If it is not spent, it seems that it must be saved. This is not quite Quesnay's position, but very close to it. Quesnay maintains that most of the indirect tax levies never did find their way into government coffers because indirect taxes burden the economy with collection costs of $250, waste of $56, and $73 *repompement*.[171] Thus indirect taxes of $500 actually bring the sovereign only $121; $379 are lost. But what happens to the $121 collected by the sovereign by means of indirect taxes? Expenditure of this money is missing from Figure #6-6. If the sovereign spends this $121, output would increase by twice this

---

[170] Ibid., p. 190.

[171] This is in essence a tax on tax. It represent the indirect taxes paid by the state as a result of spending by the sovereign. The figure of $73 is derived by multiplying state spending of $800 ($300 coming from direct taxes on the proprietors and $500 coming from indirect taxes) by the 9% tax. $73 is arrived at rather than $72 because Quesnay subdivides the $500 indirect tax receipts into two components of $250 each. When he computes the 9% tax on each $250 he rounds $22.50 up to $23. Needless to say, since Quesnay does not have the state spend its tax revenues, and since he claims that a large portion of indirect taxes is lost through collection costs and waste, the additional inclusion of a *répompement* of $73 must be attributed to an over-whelming zeal on the part of Quesnay to demonstrate the costs of indirect taxes.

amount in both the manufacturing and agricultural sectors. We should also consider what happens to the tax collection costs of $250. These government costs are someone's income. As long as the income is not saved, this $250 should be spent on manufactured and agricultural goods, which in turn should generate incomes to be spent by the producing classes. The reason this money is not part of the *Tableau* must be that Quesnay thinks the costs of collecting indirect taxes wind up being saved. At the end of "The Second Economic Problem" Quesnay almost says just this. He identifies several "other damages" resulting from indirect taxation. The second damage is that "monetary fortunes...are increased by the profits of financiers who farm out the indirect taxes, and which check or upset the circulation of money and prevent its annual return to agriculture."[172] Quesnay's position is clearer in part VI of *L'Ami des Hommes*. There he maintains that taxation *is* forced savings. Consequently, it stops work, extinguishes reproduction, and leads to the ruin of a nation.[173] The argument of "The Second Economic Problem" then seems to be that indirect taxation results in savings.[174] Direct taxes, in contrast, are collected by the sovereign, who spends the entire amount of the tax collected. We saw earlier in this chapter the effects of the savings. Direct taxes since they result in no hoarding, have no effect on reproduction. Indirect taxes, since they are saved, lead to a decline in annual reproduction.

It is clear that Quesnay has begged the question here. Assuming that only indirect taxation are hoarded, only indirect taxes

---

[172] Meek, *Economics of Physiocracy*, p. 193.

[173] Mirabeau and Quesnay, *L'Ami des Hommes*, Vol. V, p. 121f. In *L'Ami des Hommes* economic decline due to a tax on the farmers is explained also in other ways. The tax causes farmers to spend less on beasts. This reduces productivity in agriculture (p. 75). Also, in contrast to "The Second Economic Problem," where the tax is ultimately borne by the proprietors, taxation in *L'Ami des Hommes* causes agriculture advances to fall (pp. 78, 120). This reduction in inputs means less output will be produced in the future (given unchanging productivity in agriculture). Finally, the *Tableau* Quesnay provides in *L'Ami des Hommes* that shows the actual decline relies upon none of these factors. Rather, the *Tableau* shows decline to be a consequence of the fact that all tax monies collected are spent on manufactured goods. Figure #2-4 demonstrates this argument. Of course, this begs the question against indirect taxes also, albeit in a different manner.

[174] We saw in Chapter II that this was also Quesnay's argument in *Philosophie Rurale*. As Figure #2-8 shows, taxes are taken away from the receipts of both producing sectors. Were this money spent, receipts would increase by the amount of the spending, and there would be no decline.

will lead to economic decline. But it is not the taxes that lead to a decline; rather it is the fact collected taxes are not spent. The Physiocratic doctrine of a unique tax on the proprietors remains unsubstantiated. Its assumptions were not clearly set forth, and its conclusions were not adequately demonstrated by Quesnay or any of this Physiocratic followers. Meek's observation that Quesnay abandoned logic for obfuscation in his enthusiasm to prove a particular proposition concerning taxation is certainly on the mark.

SECTION IV

Finally, a brief note on Quesnay and the business cycle. This seems in order because the *Tableau* contains the seeds of a very unusual variety of business cycle theory. Moreover, neither Quesnay, not subsequent commentators on the *Tableau* have recognized this potential application of the *Tableau*.

Innovation in agriculture and savings, or underconsumption, lead to growth and decline in the *Tableau*. But so does a factor virtually ignored in the 230 years since the third edition of the *Tableau* was published. This factor is *mis*consumption, and it is the effects of consuming different sorts of goods that lead to an interesting business cycle theory.

We have already seen how an increased propensity to consume manufactured, rather than agricultural, goods leads to economic decline, and how an increased propensity to consume agricultural goods results in economic growth. One cause of upswings and downturns in economic activity are this the propensity to consume food and manufactured goods.

This is as far as Quesnay progresses in developing a theory of the business cycle however. He does not see the turning points which would have resulted in a complete theory of the business cycle. Such turning points, however, are not difficult to discern. Let us consider what happens as all classes consume more manufactured goods and fewer agricultural goods. The agricultural surplus declines, and so too do proprietor rents. As proprietor rents fall, the per capita consumption of the proprietors must also decline. It is assumed that the two producing classes receive subsistence wages. For the manufacturing sector this was $500 food and $500 manufactured goods. It was also assumed by Quesnay that the population of the manufacturing class was the same as the population of the proprietary class. Thus when proprietor incomes drop to

$1000 they too are consuming at subsistence levels.

When revenues drop again, proprietors' per capita consumption falls below subsistence. As landowners cannot migrate to another country where proprietor per capita consumption is higher, the population mechanism of Chapter IV is inapplicable to the proprietors. If they do not emigrate, they must cut their consumption. But what consumption is to be cut? If they are already consuming food at subsistence levels, it will not be possible to reduce food consumption. Only the consumption of luxury, manufactured goods can be cut. But this must increase the propensity to consume agricultural goods. In the next productive period, the economy will expand because of the increased consumption of agricultural goods. A boom phase in the cycle begins. As the economy grows, proprietor rents increase. But with high rents and a high rents and a high propensity to consume agricultural goods, proprietors begin consuming large quantities of food. A satiation point will be reached eventually. Expenditure on agricultural goods beyond this satiation point will lead to waste of agricultural goods. So when a satiation level is reached, additional income or revenues will have to go to purchasing manufactured goods. This increases the propensity to consume manufactured goods and reduces the propensity to consume agricultural goods. If, as Quesnay assumed, the behavior of the proprietors is followed by the producing classes, the additional expenditure on manufactured goods will result in economic decline. Our second turning point in the cycle has been rounded.

Again, it is important to note that this application of the *Tableau* was not recognized by Quesnay. But it is consistent with Quesnay's assumption and is a logical extension of the *Tableau*'s economic analysis. It also points to the fact the *Tableau* is an extraordinarily rich tool for seeking to understand the workings of an economy and the effects of economic policy and other changes on economic growth.

CHAPTER VII
AN EVALUATION OF TIIE *TABLEAU*

Let's briefly recapitulate the preceding exposition. Chapter II examined how Quesnay struggled to develop the *Tableau*. Quesnay's vision of a circular flow took form when he sat down to sketch the relations between society's classes. The map Quesnay drew for himself was the *Tableau Économique*, the first economic model. We saw how Quesnay modified his presentation of the *Tableau*, and that between publication of the second and third editions he came to realize that the *Tableau* could be used to show economic growth and decline as well as simple reproduction. These dynamic *Tableaux* then became Quesnay's major concern. By isolating factors leading to growth and decline Quesnay was able to use his model to analyze policy effects, and thereby provide economic arguments for and against various policy proposals.

Chapter III examined the static version of the *Tableau*. Using a sequence of tables, the assumptions and mechanics of the *Tableau* were set forth. Special attention was paid to the role of foreign trade, since the *Tableau* appeared to require all nations to export food and import manufactured goods, clearly an impossibility. Several ways out of this were discovered, thus closing Quesnay's model and demonstrating that a satisfactory reconstruction of the *Tableau* could be given. Finally, the relationships, between the zig-zag, formula, and tabular presentations of the *Tableau* were explored.

Chapter IV looked at dynamic versions of the *Tableau*. The assumptions and mechanisms of this model were set forth and the operation of the model explained. The key mechanism was found to be the change in population caused by a change in demand. It is this which prevents a sector's inputs from becoming depleted when demand for its output rises.

The relationship between the *Tableau* and input-output analysis was the subject of Chapter V. The *Tableau* was first put into input-output format. Then the similarities and differences between these models were examined more carefully. While several common factors were identified, it was argued that the *Tableau* contains features that make it incompatible with input-output tables.

163

Exchange in the *Tableau* takes place sequentially; all input-output transactions are assumed to take place simultaneously. By abstracting from real time, input-output analysis is more like Walrasian equilibrium models than the *Tableau*. In addition, input-output models are unable to show the dynamics of economic growth and decline. Finally, the notion of rent is viewed differently by the respective models. Rent is an input or factor payment for rental services in input-output models. In the *Tableau*, on the other hand, inputs are commodities. Rent can only be an habitual payment stemming from feudal traditions, or, an expropriation of surplus value by the proprietors.

Finally, in Chapter VI we looked at Quesnay's attempts to analyze the effects of hoarding, price changes, and indirect taxes using the *Tableau*. In the first two instances Quesnay's arguments and analysis were shown to be more or less correct given his assumptions. High prices for agricultural goods stimulate the economy (due to the fact that rental payments to proprietors increase with a lag); while hoarding causes an economy to decline. Quesnay's views on taxation however were found wanting. His argument was shown to depend upon the assumption that direct taxes collected by the sovereign would be spent, whereas indirect taxes are always saved. Since indirect taxes are hoarded, economic decline must result from this sort of tax. This, unfortunately, begs the question in favor of the Physiocrats' tax policy—a unique, direct tax placed on the proprietors.

We shall conclude now with an evaluation of the *Tableau*. The clarity and consistency of the *Tableau* as a mathematical model has already been demonstrated. This answers many critics of the model. However, the *Tableau* has also been attacked for conflicting with the world it models. Section I looks at these so-called contradictions. The *Tableau* has also been greatly praised. Mainly this praise has been for the influence of the *Tableau* on modern forms of analysis and for the novelties introduced by Quesnay. Section II examines this praise. Finally, in Section III, I present my own evaluation of Quesnay's remarkable model.

SECTION I

Over the years, Quesnay's economic vision, as well as his model, have come under attack. Attacks on Quesnay's vision involve broader issues than the consistency of his model. They concern the overarching assumptions of the *Tableau*; and whether such assumptions are internally consistent and conform with social, economic, and political realities.

It was Marx who first noted problems with the *Tableau*'s presuppositions. He called these "contradictions of the Physiocrat's system" and devoted a section of *Theories of Surplus Value* to discussing them.[175]

A first problem involves the nature of the economy modeled. In one sense, Marx notes, the *Tableau* describes a feudal reproductive system dominated by the landed proprietors. On this interpretation the manufacturing sector or industrial sphere, which is where capitalism first develops historically, is a mere appendage to agriculture and the feudal relations between landlord and tenant farmer. In another sense, though, the *Tableau* analyzes capitalist production. Conditions for the production and accumulation of capital are set out. A class called "productive" creates surplus value by laboring on the land. This is then expropriated by a class called "the proprietors." Despite these misleading names, the relations between "the productive class" and "the proprietors" identifies them as a laboring class and a capitalist class respectively. Production, as such, is capitalist production. The contradiction here, according to Marx, is that "feudalism is...portrayed and explained from the viewpoint of bourgeois production."[176]

From the perspective of a fully developed capitalism, where industry dominates, what Marx says makes sense. Quesnay does describe what we now recognize as capitalist production relations. To say that this was Quesnay's intent is quite another matter though. Quesnay's knowledge of capitalism was surely limited; and what is described in the *Tableau* must be taken to be the economy most familiar to him—a "feudal" economy. The fact that the *Tableau* can also be viewed as a description and analysis of capitalist production points to the fact that an important phenomenon—the creation and expropriation of surplus value—is shared by two socio-economic formations. But this does not demonstrate a contradiction in Quesnay's vision of the economic process.

Marx finds a second contradiction in the Physiocratic notion of net product. On the one hand, the Physiocrats viewed this surplus

---

[175] Karl Marx, *Theories of Surplus Value* (Moscow: Foreign Language Publishing House, 1954). Section 2 of Chapter 2 is devoted to this topic.

[176] Ibid., p. 49f.

as a gift of nature. This is why surpluses arise only in agriculture.
But the Physiocrats also viewed the surplus as resulting from the
production and exchange relations between the landlord-capitalist
and the workers. Exchanging the use of his land for labor power,
the landlord-capitalist is able to exact as a return any surplus output.
So, while Marx praises Quesnay for being the first to see surplus
value as the appropriation of another's labor, he criticizes Quesnay
for considering surplus value as expropriated labor *and* as a gift of
nature. "On the one hand, it stripped rent...of its feudal wrapping,
and reduced it to mere surplus value in excess of the laborers' wage.
On the other hand, this surplus value is explained again in a feudal
way, as derived from nature and not from society; from man's
relation to the soil and not from his social relationships."[177]

Marx is correct here that the Physiocratic notion of net
product is multi-faceted. But he is wrong in believing that this
reveals an inconsistency on Quesnay's part. In fact, Quesnay
probably held neither of the two positions on the net product that
Marx attributes to him. Land for Quesnay was only a possible source
of surplus; it is necessary, but not a necessary and sufficient condition
for the creation of surplus value. Unworked land certainly yields no
surplus. Similarly, the manner in which the land is farmed
determines the amount of the net product. *Grande agriculture*
yielded greater surpluses than *petite agriculture.* The view that for
Quesnay the net product is merely a gift of nature is therefore too
simple. The net product is neither exclusively a direct gift of nature
nor exclusively a result of exchanges between cultivator and
proprietor; rather it is the consequence of several variables, whose
interaction results in its creation.

Finally, Marx finds problems in the Physiocratic attitude
toward property. Quesnay venerates landed property; yet the
Physiocrats all demanded that taxes be placed solely on the
proprietors. Such taxation is a negation of property rights according
to Marx. "Landed property is in part confiscated."[178]

Here Marx imputes a contradiction to Quesnay by
misreading him. Taxation was not viewed as confiscation by
Quesnay. Instead taxes were necessary for the state to fulfill its social
role. The tax monies collected by the sovereign had to be devoted

---

[177] Ibid., p. 51f.
[178] Ibid., p. 52.

to socially important purposes. Quesnay argued for a direct tax on the proprietors because he thought this was the least costly way to raise revenues and believed taxes must fall on the proprietors if the economy is not to decline. A tax on land is thus justified on the grounds of economic efficiency. Moreover, as Einaudi has argued, the net product was not viewed by the Physiocrats as the property of the proprietors. It was a national dividend. Taxation was then a matter of dividing this dividend between the landowner and the sovereign. And even this division had to be kept within rational limits. If the state took too large a portion of this dividend, taxation would become a burden on the state and disaster would follow.[179]

Gide and Rist[180] and Elizabeth Fox-Genovese[181] have also maintained that Quesnay's system contains several contradictions. For Gide and Rist the central problem in Physiocracy revolves around the net product. In contrast to Marx, Gide and Rist find a contradiction in the Physiocrat's view that on the one hand the net product was a gift of nature, and on the other hand the proprietor must perform several functions in exchange for the net product. "If the revenue which the proprietor draws represents the remuneration for his outlay...the net product vanishes."[182] Gide and Rist then go on to identify five duties that the proprietors must perform.[183]

(1) They must bring lands into cultivation; that is, they must provide *advances foncières*.

(2) They must dispose of their revenues in a manner that promotes the general interest. This means they must not hoard any part of their revenues and must spend at least half their revenues on agricultural goods.

(3) They must provide public services.[184]

---

[179] Luigi Einaudi, "The Physiocratic Theory of Taxation," in *Economic Essays in Honour of Gustav Cassel* (London: Frank Cass & Co., 1967), p. 132.

[180] Charles Gide and Charles Rist, *A History of Economic Doctrines* (Boston: D.C. Heath and Company, 1949).

[181] Elizabeth Fox-Genovese, *The Origins of Physiocracy* (Ithaca: Cornell University Press, 1976).

[182] Gide and Rist, *A History of Economic Doctrines*, p. 43.

[183] Ibid., p. 44.

[184] As Einaudi, "The Physiocratic Theory of Taxation," points out, the producing classes of society are too busy producing to have much time for public service. Only the proprietors have the requisite leisure time.

(4)   They must bear the entire burden of taxation.
(5)   They must be careful not demand more than the
           value of the net product as rental incomes.

The rent which the proprietor receives according to Gide
and Rist is a factor payment for performing these duties. It is part
of the gross agricultural output to be divided up among those
contributing to its production. As such, it cannot be a gift of nature,
for a gift is not a factor payment received in exchange for services
rendered.

Gide and Rist's view of proprietor rents dovetails with that of
input-output reconstructions of the *Tableau*. In Chapter V we saw
that input-output tables could account for the output of a sector only
by means of inputs with equal value. The agricultural surplus
created a problem. Agricultural output was greater than the value
of agricultural inputs. Input-output reconstructions dealt with this
problem by making proprietor revenues a factor payment. This
increased the value of inputs to the point where they just equaled the
value of output. We also saw in Chapter V that this view imputed to
Quesnay a position he would have rejected. Production for Quesnay
was by means of commodities rather than by means of factors of
production. Proprietor services cannot be inputs for Quesnay. Thus
there can be no conflict between the notion of the net product and
the services performed by the proprietors. It is only when things are
viewed from neoclassical spectacles that a problem arises. But when
the *Tableau* is understood as it was intended, when it is considered
in its proper historical context, Gide and Rist's contradiction vanishes.
Moreover, even if rent were a factor payment it is hard to justify the
amount of the payment. It should be remembered that per capita
income for the proprietors is twice that of the agricultural class. To
justify this based upon their contributions to production such as
bearing the tax burden and spending all their income, half on
manufactured goods and half on agriculture, seems rather silly.

Finally, for Elizabeth Fox-Genovese contradictions in
Physiocracy also "arise primarily from the social, political and
ideological context of the endeavor."[185] A first problem, the uneasy
tension between the capitalist and feudal elements of Quesnay's

---

[185] Fox-Genovese, *The Origins of Physiocracy*, p. 300.

model,[186] is identical to one of the problems spotted by Marx. Having just dealt with this issue, no further comment seems in order here.

Of greater interest is the contradiction Fox-Genovese notes between the proscriptive and descriptive elements of Quesnay's model. The *Tableau*, she claims, was not meant to be a description of the French economy in the middle of the 18th century. On the contrary, it depicted circulation and production relationships in an ideal world, one which would come into existence following adoption of Physiocratic reforms. But these changes, Fox-Genovese argues, are likely to require social political readjustments,[187] and reforms will have to be put into effect by those opposed to such reforms. For example, agriculture is supposed to be modernized. In fact, when the Physiocratic policies adopted in 1763 and 1764 failed to produce the hoped for results, the Physiocrats themselves argued that the failure stemmed from insufficient cooperation on the part of the proprietors. As a second instance of Fox-Genovese's point we can consider taxes. The Physiocrats maintained taxes should be placed only on the proprietors. Yet, as Quesnay notes in "The Second Economic Problem," the proprietors will oppose this and force the state to impose indirect taxes as well. Freedom of trade in grain and freedom to work where one wanted are additional Physiocratic proscriptions that conflicted with established political powers. These freedoms would have meant the end to the despotism of the *ancien regime*.[188] The problem here is that Quesnay fails to explain how the freedoms he advocates could come into existence over the entrenched power of the monarchy. Yet, without these freedoms, the *Tableau* as an economic model would be inoperative.

Fox-Genovese's criticisms do point to a genuine and fundamental problem with *Tableau*—namely a conflict between the economic assumptions of the model and the social and political superstructure within which the model is supposed to operate.

It should be kept in mind here, however, that this is not a problem with just the *Tableau*, but a trap for all economic models. Economic models express relations between economic variables. They are manipulated by changing the value of one variable and noting the effect of this change on other variables. An important

---

[186] Ibid., p. 294.

[187] Ibid., p. 98.

[188] Ibid., p. 21ff.

feature of the enterprise, which gets overlooked due to a fascination with the purely economic variables, is the positing of a set of social and political institutions and habits that are invariant with respect to changes in economic variables. This is always hidden in the economist's famous *ceteris paribus* assumption. What gets ignored as a result is the relation between the economic variables of the model and the social and political climate in which the model operates. Any effect of the economy on this superstructure and any feedback from the superstructure to the economy is not taken into account.

Quesnay has thus not freed himself from what has become the economist's disease—a fascination with economic models that abstract from socio-economic conditions of the real world. In fact, Quesnay may be regarded as the first victim of this disease, since his *Tableau* was the first economic model. These criticisms, though, do not detract from the important contributions made by the *Tableau* and the lasting influence of Quesnay. Nor do they negate the brilliance of the *Tableau*. It is to these issues that we now turn.

SECTION II

Praise for the *Tableau* has usually been for anticipating contemporary economic notions and modes of analysis. The idea of economic life as a circular flow is an obvious novelty introduced by Quesnay, which a number of commentators have picked up on. Ignoring the *Tableau*, Elizabeth Fox-Genovese maintains this is one of the central contributions of Quesnay.[189] A like opinion is expressed by Schumpeter in *Economic Doctrine and Method*[190] and by Blaug. Blaug also includes Quesnay's discovery of the notion of reproduction and his formulation of the distinction between productive and unproductive labor as among his significant contributions to economics.[191] In a similar vein, Marx singles out three contributions of the Physiocrats for special praise. Their understanding of capital, Marx thought, merited commendation. They developed the notion of circulating capital, or advances, as a

---

[189] Ibid., p. 50f.

[190] Joseph A. Schumpeter, *Economic Doctrine and Method* (New York: Oxford University Press, 1954), p. 52.

[191] Mark Blaug, *Economic Theory in Retrospect*, 3rd ed. (Cambridge: Cambridge University Press, 1978), p. 24.

wage fund; they distinguished fixed from circulating capital; and they established the connection between the circulation of capital and the reproduction process of capital.[192] A second contribution is the Physiocrats' understanding of how surplus value is created. Embedded in the *Tableau* is the recognition that only productive labor creates surplus value. The third and, according to Marx, the greatest contribution of the Physiocrats was their analysis and inquiry into the nature of surplus value. Surplus value, the Physiocrats correctly saw, originated in production rather than in circulation. By discovering this principle, Marx said, the Physiocrats "thereby laid the foundation for the analysis of capitalist production."[193]

Of greater interest are comparisons of the *Tableau* with later economic models. Meek concludes his essay "Problems of the *Tableau Économique*" by noting four parallels between the *Tableau* and modern methods of economic analysis. Foreshadowing these modern modes of analysis he regards as the major contribution of the *Tableau*.

First, Meek notes that the *Tableau* contains elements of a Walrasian equilibrium system. This parallel has been remarked upon by other commentators as well. Schumpeter, for example, writes that the *Tableau* "was the first method ever devised in order to convey an explicit conception of the nature of economic equilibrium."[194] Certainly this is true of the static *Tableau*. This *Tableau* is comprised of a number of different sectors and markets, all of which must be in equilibrium if the entire model is to be in equilibrium. This is also true of a Walrasian general equilibrium system; and on this level there are obvious similarities between the *Tableau* and general equilibrium models. However, these parallels are not exact, and do not hold up under closer examination.

One difference between the *Tableau* and general equilibrium models has to do with the notion of time. General equilibrium models are timeless. All exchanges—the exchange of endowments for money incomes and the exchange of money incomes for produced goods and services—take place at once following the establishment of a set of equilibrium prices by some *tâtonnement* process. There is no recognition that some order in the exchange

---

[192] Marx, *Theories of Surplus Value*, p. 44.
[193] Ibid., p. 45.
[194] Joseph A. Schumpeter, *History of Economic Analysis* (New York: Oxford University Press, 1954), p. 242.

process may be necessary—that some exchanges must take place before others, or that production must occur before goods are consumed. In contrast, we have seen that the *Tableau* takes cognizance of the fact that production and distribution occur at different times and that exchange is sequential rather than simultaneous. Quesnay's model had to take account of time because according to the model production requires the prior accumulation of capital. This feature gives the *Tableau* a realism that is lacking from general equilibrium descriptions of the reproduction process.

A more important difference arises from the fact that general equilibrium models are self-correcting models. Excess demand in some market must be accompanied by lack of demand in some other market, and vice versa. Markets experiencing increases in demand attract resources because their prices rise and returns to suppliers increase. These markets consequently expand. Meanwhile those markets experiencing reduced demand will contract, as unsold goods tend to lower prices and returns to the supplier. As such, all markets tend towards equilibrium.

Quesnay did not believe there were self-correcting forces in the economy and did not include in the *Tableau* any self-adjusting mechanism that would move the entire system to an equilibrium position. Quite the contrary, the *Tableau* was used to demonstrate that if there was excess expenditure on manufactured goods and insufficient expenditure on agricultural goods the economy would decline and would continue to decline. The only thing that could change this situation would be a change in spending propensities favoring agricultural goods.

In addition, Quesnay thought that taxes placed improperly on agricultural advances would lead to a decline that would be reversible only by putting the tax on proprietor revenues. There is nothing about improper taxation which unleashes forces within the economy to stop and reverse this decline. Nor does the *Tableau* contain a mechanism by which improper taxes will eventually lead the sovereign to change the way it taxes its citizens.

Finally, the argument in "The First Economic Problem" was that price changes cause economic growth and decline. An increase in price will lead to continual increases in annual reproduction, while a price reduction will result in progressive decline. Again, there is nothing in the *Tableau* to halt this process of growth or decline.[195] Once output begins to increase, proprietor rents, and demand, both rise. The increased demand perpetuates the growth process, which is soon reinforced by increased productivity in agriculture. Growth accelerates; there is no feedback mechanism to restrain the process once it begins. A similar process will tend to perpetuate economic decline. Thus, the *Tableau* and Walrasian general equilibrium models differ in one very important respect. General equilibrium, but not the *Tableau*, contains a self-correcting capacity. To the extent that the real world economy is not self-correcting, but evinces protracted periods of expansion and contraction, the *Tableau* must be judged the more realistic, and hence superior, model.

At the end of Chapter VI the *Tableau* was made into a cyclical model through having reductions in output result in changes in spending propensities that tend to stop decline and restrain growth. This assumption was not in Quesnay, but even its inclusion in the *Tableau* leaves a vast gulf between the *Tableau* and general equilibrium models. For the state of the economy will depend on when spending propensities change back to a 50-50 split between agricultural and manufactured goods (assuming no savings). If this occurs early, when the economy just begins to decline, output will decline only a little. However, if this occurs at a late stage in the process of decline static equilibrium will be attained at significantly lower levels of output. In both instance, however, the economy does decline; in general equilibrium models such a decline could not take place.

A second parallel Meek discusses is that between the *Tableau* and Keynesian economic models. There are a number of points at which these two models are similar. Both are concerned with economic aggregates and with factors that cause aggregate output to decline. Keynesian models focus on investment as the key variable for understanding economic decline; the focus in the *Tableau* is on improper spending propensities, excessive savings, and improper taxation. Investment, however, is not ignored in the *Tableau*. Investment in agriculture is important as a stimulus to productivity improvements, and as such, a key stimulus to economic growth.

---

[195] This is not exactly true. In *L'Ami des Hommes* Quesnay recognizes that there are limits to the availability and fruitfulness of land. When these limits are approached, growth must come to an end. See Victor de Riquetti, Marquis de Mirabeau and Francois Quesnay, *L'Ami des Hommes* (Avignon, 1962), Vol. V, p. 68.

Meek also notes that both Quesnay and Keynes cite faulty government policy as a reason for poor economic performance, and that there are a number of similarities between Quesnay's zig-zags and the Keynesian multiplier. We saw in Chapter IV that the propensities to consume agricultural and manufactured goods (along with proprietor incomes) determine the output of agricultural and manufactured commodities. This is certainly similar to the determination of gross national product in Keynesian models given the marginal propensity to consume as part of a consumption function. Finally, we saw in Chapter VI that savings by any of the three classes of society results in the impoverishment of the nation. Recognition of the malevolent economic effects of savings virtually disappears from economics until it is resuscitated by Keynes as the famous paradox of thrift.

The third similarity that Meek notes is between the *Tableau* and modern dynamic methods of analysis. However, Meek does not think the parallel here is close. The general method of the *Tableau*, he believes, is closer to comparative statics than to modern dynamic analysis. Unfortunately, Meek says little more on this point. Moreover, he misses several truly important and interesting parallel between the *Tableau* and modern dynamic theories of economic growth. In particular, the similarities between the results Quesnay derived using the *Tableau* and the results of the Harrod and Domar models are striking.[196] Since this is not a work on contemporary models of economic growth, I will only summarize the main results of the Harrod and Domar models. These results have come to be known as the "First and Second Harrod Problems."

The First Harrod Problem is a dynamic version of the Keynesian argument that capitalist economies may achieve equilibrium at less than full employment. Harrod proves that a similar proposition holds true of growing economies—there is no reason to assume a capitalist economy will grow at the right rate to

---

[196] On the Harrod model see Roy F. Harrod, "An Essay in Dynamic Theory," *Economic Journal* 49 (1939), 14-33 and Roy F. Harrod, *Towards a Dynamic Economics* (London: Macmillan, 1948). Domar's model is presented in E.D. Domar, "Capital Expansion, Rate of Growth and Employment," *American Economic Review* 37 (1947), 34-44. A good summary of the models and a comparison of the similarities between the Harrod and Domar models is contained in Hywel G. Jones, *An Introduction to Modern Theories of Economic Growth* (New York: McGraw Hill, 1976), pp. 40-65.

maintain full employment. The similarities between this proposition and the *Tableau* are minimal. The notion of a warranted rate of growth does not appear in the *Tableau*. Moreover, for Quesnay, the growth of the labor force was an endogenous rather than an exogenous variable. Its value was determined by the level of output—by how many workers the nation's output will enable to subsist—rather than by biological forces. A general concern with economic growth and recognition of the possibility that equilibrium may be at less than full employment are the only real similarities here.

Things are different with respect to the Second Harrod Problem. This is usually referred to as the knife-edge problem, because Harrod's results show that divergences of the actual rate of growth, G_a, and the warranted rate of growth, G_w, are not self-correcting. Rather, any divergence will lead to even greater divergences. The economy is perched on a knife-edge because only at the point of this edge, where $G_a = G_w$, is steady growth possible. All other points result in either continuous expansion or continuous contraction.

This property of growing economies had its origin in the *Tableau*. We saw the effect of savings propensities on the economy in Chapter IV. Reproduction continues at the same level of output in the *Tableau* if and only if all classes spend half their incomes on manufactured goods and half on agricultural goods.[197] This is the edge to Quesnay's knife. If the propensity to consume manufactured goods equals the propensity to consume agricultural goods the economy remains perched on this point. Quesnay does not say it is unlikely for an economy to remain there. In fact, Quesnay seems to hope and believe that with the proper economic policies and with the right habits and customs instilled in the population a position of static equilibrium could be attained. The likelihood of all classes consuming goods in exactly the necessary proportions, however, must be low. Were an economy in static equilibrium it would have to be considered serendipitous. What is most striking though is that the effect of unequal consumption propensities in the *Tableau* is precisely the effect of unequal growth rates in Harrod's model. If the propensity to consume manufactured goods is greater than the propensity to consume agricultural goods the economy declines. The

---

[197] Or if the proprietors' spending propensities are the reverse of the propensities of the two producing classes. Quesnay, however, did not see that this was a possible means to get back on the edge of the knife.

decline is not self-adjusting, but continuous. As less agricultural goods are demanded, less are grown, and a smaller surplus is produced. This decreases proprietor revenues and demand in succeeding periods, thus leading to further declines. On the other hand, if the propensity to consume manufactured goods is less than the propensity to consume agricultural goods, the economy expands and continues to do so. Again, as in Harrod, expansion continues unabated.

Finally, Meek's fourth and last parallel between the *Tableau* and modern forms of analysis involves Leontief's input-output analysis. Meek, however, agrees with arguments of Chapter V that despite some superficial similarities, the parallel between input-output analysis and the *Tableau* is not very pronounced. He notes that Quesnay would have "raised his eyebrows at this model, which effectively conceals the difference between the surplus-producing capacity of the productive class and that of the sterile class, and obliges us to assume that the proprietors produce 'rental services' in return for their revenue" and concludes that the similarities are insignificant here since the Physiocratic aggregates can be translated into any equilibrium model involving aggregates, given a few modifications in the *Tableau*'s assumptions.[198]

Meek has not been the only one to praise the *Tableau* for foreshadowing modern methods of analysis. In Volume II of *Capital* Marx singles out the *Tableau* as being the precursor of his simple reproduction model.[199] Marx left it to the reader, however, to draw out the relationship between his model and the *Tableau*. Recently, Shigeto Tsuru has taken a step in this direction.[200] Tsuru's efforts are worth examining and expanding upon here.

We begin with some of the more superficial similarities between the static *Tableau* and Marx's simple reproduction model. The use and emphasis upon sector or class analysis is characteristic shared by both models. Sets of individuals are grouped together based upon the similar functions they perform within the economy. Different sets of individuals are regarded as different economic classes, and relationships between the classes becomes a focus of

---

[198] Meek, *Economics of Physiocracy*, p. 295.

[199] Karl Marx, *Capital*, Volume II (New York: International Publishers, 1967), p. 359ff.

[200] Shigeto Tsuru, "On Reproduction Schemes," in Paul M. Sweezy, *The Theory of Capitalist Development* (New York: Monthly Review, 1942), pp. 365-74.

economic analysis. This approach contrasts markedly with contemporary, neoclassical models. There, the focus is on the single, autonomous, and independent individual. Each individual is regarded as a utility maximizer rather than as a member of some class performing a function as part of the reproduction process. Moreover, it is assumed that each individual's utility is independent of the utilities of everybody else.[201] The possible development of mutual class interests or a class consciousness is thus ruled out *ex hypotheses* by neoclassical analysis, but constitutes an important aspect of the economic theories of Quesnay and the classical economists.

We have already examined the issue of the origin of surplus value. The *Tableau* places this solely in the realm of production. This is also true of Marx's simple reduction schema. In this model, the output of a given sector, w_i, is divided into three components: surplus value, constant capital, and variable capital. Thus we have Marx's simple reproduction equation:

$$w_i = s_i + c_i + v_i$$

Constant capital, c_i, is the value of materials used up in production and the depreciation of capital; variable capital, v_i, is the capital that must be paid to the worker as subsistence during the productive process, and s_i, is surplus value. The important point to note here is that nothing has been said about exchange. Surplus value arises solely in the realm of production and it arises because the output produced by the laborer in the course of a day's work is greater than the output that the worker needs to subsist and reproduce another generation of workers.

Again, the contrast between the views of Quesnay and Marx on the one hand, and contemporary views is striking. In neoclassical models, value is defined in terms of a psychological trait—utility—and so consequently it gets divorced from the production process. Individuals can increase their utility by either of two means. First, they can revalue their preferences. This possibility is usually eliminated in neoclassical models by the assumption that individual preferences are fixed and do not change as other variables in the model change. But even if changes in utility were allowed,

---

[201] For an interesting discussion of this assumption see Harvey Leibstein, *Beyond Economic Man: A New Foundation for Microeconomics* (Cambridge: Cambridge University Press, 1976).

additional value would not arise in the production of commodities. Instead it would arise in the psychological sphere and be grounded in the individual's evaluation of utility. A second means of creating surplus value in a neoclassical model is for an individual, i, to trade some good A for another good B, where the utility of B for i is greater than the utility of A for i. Exchange in this case increases i's total utility. And since value is utility in this model, surplus value had been created. We can also assume that the individual j, who gets A and gives up B, must also experience additional utility. Otherwise j would not exchange B for A. Exchange then, and *not* production, is the means by which surplus value is created in a neoclassical model. By employing a class or sectoral analysis and by finding the origin of surplus value in production relations, Quesnay clearly deserves a place in the classical school of economic thought.

A third similarity between Marx's simple reproduction model and the *Tableau* concerns the accumulation of capital. For both Marx and Quesnay it is accumulated capital which makes an economic system run. Capital accumulation in agriculture is necessary to modernize agriculture in the *Tableau*. This increases original advances in agriculture and allows the cultivators of the land to employ more modern agricultural methods. It is this capital that generates greater surpluses. In the *Tableau*, however, additional surpluses are not used to increase the stock of capital; they are not accumulated. Surplus value gets paid to the proprietor and is used for additional consumption. This constitutes the feudal aspect of the *Tableau*, and distinguishes it from Marx's analysis of capitalist production.

The absence of a self-correcting mechanism is another similarity between the *Tableau* and Marx's simple reproduction model. In both models the economy is subject to crises that do not end as a result of natural, systemic tendencies. These properties of the *Tableau* were discussed in contrasting it with Walrasian equilibrium models. On this issue, Marx clearly sides with Quesnay. Although he does not consider improper consumption as a cause of crises, Marx recognized savings, or the decision of capitalists to postpone investment, and improper taxation, which reduces profit rates and leads the capitalist to increase exploitation of the worker, as factors that might precipitate a crisis.

In a previously published paper[202] I argued that the *Tableau* shares a number of similarities with Kaldor's growth theory. First, both Kaldor and Quesnay argue for the special status of one economic sector. It is agriculture that possesses dynamic features for Quesnay and manufacturing that is dynamic for Kaldor. Yet, for both of them, the growth of that dynamic sector causes overall economic growth. Moreover, this relationship, does not work in reverse. The growth of non-manufacturing sectors does not spur economic growth according to Kaldor's laws. Similarly, we have seen that for Quesnay relative growth of the sterile sector actually causes economic contraction.

A second parellel between Kaldor and Quesnay is that increasing returns provides the key mechanism in their growth theories. Following the argument of Allan Young, Kaldor maintains that the growth of manufacturing leads to economies of scale from increased differentiation and the process of "learning by doing."[203] We have seen previously that faster growth permits the transition from "petite" to "grande" agriculture according to Quesnay.

Third, both Quesnay and Kaldor see the dynamic sector constrained by demand factors rather than by supply factors. We saw above that according to the *Tableau* increased demand for agricultural goods will reallocate inputs to the agricultural sector. One potential economic problem for Quesnay, is that spending, especially by wealthy proprietors, is likely to favor luxury manufactured goods. Similarly, Kaldor argued that economic growth would increase the demand for goods produced by the tertiary sector of the economy. For both Kaldor and Quesnay these spending tendencies will reduce overall economic growth unless something is done to raise demand for goods produced by the dynamic sector of the economy. Quesnay favored taxes on wealthy proprietors and state spending on agricultural goods. Kaldor favored an industrial policy where the state would provide support to the manufacturing sector, thus increasing manufactured exports and reducing the amount of imported manufactured goods.

A final modern method of analysis anticipated by the *Tableau*

---

[202] "Quesnay's Theory of Economic Growth & Decline," in *Economics as Worldly Philosophy*, ed. Ron Blackwell, Jaspal Chatha and Edward J. Nell (London: Macmillan, 1993), pp. 305-21.

[203] Nicholas Kaldor, *Strategic Factors in Economic Development* (Ithaca: Cornell University Press, 1967), p. 24.

was first mentioned by Sraffa, who contended that the *Tableau* contained the original picture of his model.[204] Gram and Walsh also seem to hold this view. They maintain that he broad characteristics of the *Tableau* "remain true of every classical model constructed subsequently down to the most recent contemporary work."[205]

Sraffian models and the *Tableau* certainly are similar in a number of respects. Both are models of the production of commodities by means of commodities; both models are able to show the existence of a surplus. Other similarities between Sraffa models and the *Tableau* are shared with input-output models and with Walrasian general equilibrium models. All these models demonstrate the viability of an economy if it produces enough output in a given year to serve as inputs for the next period's production.

However, a different view of the relation between Sraffa and Quesnay is held by Pasinetti. Pasinetti traces one line of descent in economics from the *Tableau* to Leontief's input-output models, and another from Ricardo to Sraffa.[206] The point of contrast is the main purpose of the respective models. The work of Ricardo and Sraffa is mainly theoretical according to Pasinetti, whereas Quesnay and Leontief are concerned primarily with practical issues. Sraffa was concerned with theoretical propositions concerning the distribution of income and prices. He demonstrated that given exogenously determined wages, relative prices and the rate of profit are determined by the technical conditions of production (of a standard commodity). Given wages then, relative prices and the rate of profit are determined, and so is the functional distribution of income. These are the main conclusions of Sraffa's work. The Sraffian system contains no mention of population, employment, and the factors leading to underemployment. The level of output is undetermined by the system, because the system contains no theory of output. These are the sorts of problems, though, that were of major concern to Quesnay. The prime purpose of the *Tableau* was to demonstrate how output could be increased. One of Quesnay's

---

[204] Piero Sraffa, *Production of Commodities by Means of Commodities* (Cambridge: Cambridge University Press, 1980), p. 93.

[205] Vivian Walsh and Harvey Gram, *Classical and Neoclassical Theories of General Equilibrium* (New York: Oxford University Press, 1980), p. 32f.

[206] Luigi L. Pasinetti, *Lectures on the Theory of Production* (New York: Columbia University Press, 1977), p. 32.

answers was that demand was an important factor. Demand, of course, is ignored by Sraffa. Another answer given by Quesnay was technical change. For Sraffa's system, however, technology has to be held constant to determine relative prices and the functional distribution of income. Quesnay's third answer, changes in price, we found to be vague and of questionable validity. Nonetheless, this answer could not be acceptable from Sraffa's viewpoint. First, relative prices in Sraffa's system do not depend upon the level of free trade, availability of communications, government prohibitions, etc. Rather, they are a function of given technologies of production and the wage rate. Second, given a set of relative prices in a Sraffa system, the output of the economy is still unknown. There are an infinite number of levels of output compatible with the determined set of relative prices.

Looked at the other way around, the major concern of Sraffa—relative prices—is virtually ignored by Quesnay. Moreover, while Quesnay has a definite theory of output he has no theory of value.[207] Certainly, the *Tableau* has nothing to do with the formation of relative prices, and has no theory of how the aggregate price level is determined. The *Tableau*'s figures are all given in price terms, but might as well have been given in quantities.

Pasinetti's case then appears stronger than that of either Sraffa or Walsh and Gram. There does seem to be one line of economic inquiry leading from Ricardo to Sraffa. This line has been concerned with mainly microeconomic problems—how prices are determined, how income is distributed and in general with the theory of value. Another line has been concerned with macro problems—employment and output theory. This is the line begun by Quesnay, and leads not so much to Leontief, as to Keynes. Throughout this section we have seen a large number of parallels between the *Tableau* and Keynesian and post-Keynesian analysis. These parallels stem from similar concerns and a similar focus on demand factors as

---

[207] Also see David Gleicher, "The Historical Bases of Physiocracy: An Analysis of the *Tableau Économique*," *Science and Society* 46 (Fall, 1982), p. 330. The work of Gianni Vaggi (see the references cited in the bibliography, especially *The Economics of François Quesnay*) has focused on developing Quesnay's theory of value in considerable detail. However, as I argued in my review of Vaggi's *The Economics of François Quesnay* (*History of Political Economy* 12 (Fall, 1991), 551-552) this theory of value is not consistent with the theory of output contained in the *Tableau*, and the theory of output in the *Tableau* must be regarded as having priority.

a cause of macroeconomic problems and as a solution to them.

SECTION III

Let me conclude with what I take to be the major point of this work. Chapters III and IV demonstrated the consistency of the *Tableau* both as a model of simple reproduction, demonstrating the viability of an economy, and as a model of a growing or contracting economy. Criticism of the *Tableau* for mystification has thus been shown to be unfounded. On the other hand, much of the praise for *Tableau* also seems, if not unfounded, certainly misplaced. For the truly remarkable thing about the *Tableau* is not that it foreshadowed contemporary modes of economic analysis or future economic developments, but that in its own right the *Tableau* is an extremely rich and useful model.

Implicitly the model contains a supply and demand mechanism. The supply side depends upon technology in agriculture, and the demand side is a function of the expenditures of the different classes of society. The interaction of these two forces determines the output for the economy. Hence the model contains a definite theory of output. Although the *Tableau* contains a supply and demand mechanism, it does not endow this mechanism with a self-correcting capacity. This permits the *Tableau* to be used in analyzing economic fluctuations and in tracing out the path of economic growth. In addition, the *Tableau* does not suffer from the huge loss of historical and empirical relevance as do Walrasian general equilibrium models, which also contain a supply-demand mechanism, but include, in addition, a mechanism by which the system tends to equilibrium with full utilization of resources or endowments. Finally, the *Tableau* contains an important analysis of the notion of "surplus." It explains how the surplus is generated, where it goes and how it can be augmented and diminished.

But perhaps the most enduring achievement of Quesnay is that he developed a model at a time when there were no other models in existence to serve as his guide. The mere construction of a model is a leap of the intellect, an exercise of abstraction, that deserves to rank among the most remarkable advances in the history of economic thought.

APPENDIX #1

Manufacturing sector purchases from the agricultural class will be equal to the following sequences, S_n.

$S_n = \$2000(3/5)(2/5) + \$2000(3/5)(2/5)^2 + \$2000(3/5)^2(2/5)^2 +$
$\$2000(3/5)^2(2/5)^3 + \$2000(3/5)^3(2/5)^3 + \ldots + \$2000(3/5)^{n-1}$
$(2/5)^n + \$2000(3/5)^n(2/5)^n$

This sequence can be simplied to

$$\$2000 \left[\frac{(2/5)(3/5)+(2/5)^2(3/5)}{1-(2/5)(3/5)} \right] = 884.$$

Agricultural purchases from the manufacturing sector are similar to S_n. The only difference is that the fractions "3/5" and "2/5" are reversed. Here the sequence will be

$S_n = \$2000(3/5)(2/5) + \$2000(3/5)^2(2/5) + \$2000(3/5)^2(2/5)^2 +$
$\$2000(3/5)^3(2/5)^2 + \$2000(3/5)^3(2/5)^3 + \ldots +$
$\$2000(3/5)^n(2/5)^{n-1} + \$2000(3/5)^n(2/5)^n.$

which can be simplified to

$$\$2000 \left[\frac{(2/5)(3/5)+(2/5)(3/5)^3}{1-(2/5)(3/5)} \right] = 1011.$$

APPENDIX #2

Let R= proprietor's revenue
         a= the marginal propensity to purchase manufactured goods
and   b= the marginal propensity to purchase agricultural goods
Productive sector receipts will be equal to proprietor expenditures
plus manufacturing sector expenditures on food. The former figure
will be bR and the latter a sequence S_n of the form:

$$S_n = abR + ab^2R + a^2b^2R + \dots$$

as in Appendix #1.
Multiplying by ab now,

$$S_nab = a^2b^2R + a^2b^3R + a^3b^3R + \dots$$
so,
$$S_n = \frac{abR + ab^2R}{1-ab}$$

Total agricultural sector receipts will be $bR + \dfrac{abR + ab^2R}{1-ab}$.

Total manufacturing sector receipts are equal to proprietor
expenditures plus agricultural sector expenditures on manufactured
goods. The former figure is aR and the latter a sequence, S_n, of the
form

$$S_n = abR + a^2bR + a^2b^2R + a^3b^2R + \dots$$

which by a procedure similar to the one above can be shown to sum
to
$$S_n = \frac{abR + a^2br}{1-ab}$$

Thus total manufacturing sector receipts will equal

$$aR + \frac{abR + a^2bR}{1-ab}$$

BIBLIOGRAPHY

Barna, Tibor. "Quesnay's Model of Economic Development," *European Economic Review*, 8 (December 1976), 315-338.

Barna, Tibor. "Quesnay's *Tableau* in Modern Guise," *Economic Journal*, 85 (September 1975), 485-496.

Blaug, Mark. *Economic Theory in Retrospect.* 3rd ed. Cambridge: Cambridge University Press, 1978.

Cantillon, Richard. *Essai sur la Nature du Commerce en Général.* Ed. & translated by Henry Higgs. New York: Augustus Kelley, 1964.

Domar, E.D. "Capital Expansion, Rate of Growth and Employment," *Econometrica*, 46 (April 1946), 137-147.

Domar, E.D. Expansion and Employment," *American Economic Review*, 37 (March 1947), 34-44.

Eagly, Robert V. "A Physiocratic Model of Dynamic Equilibrium," *Journal of Political Economy*, 77 (January-February 1969), 6-84.

Eagly, Robert V. *The Structure of Classical Economic Theory.* New York: Oxford University Press, 1974.

Einaudi, Luigi. "The Physiocratic Theory of Taxation," in *Economic Essays in Honor of Gustov Cassel.* London: Frank Cass & Co., 1967.

Eltis, Walter A. "François Quesnay: A Reinterpretation 1. The *Tableau Économique,*" *Oxford Economic Papers,* 27 (July 1975), 167-200.

Eltis, Walter A. "François Quesnay: A Reinterpretation 2. The Theory of Economic Growth," *Oxford Economic Papers,* 27 (November 1975), 327-351.

Engels, Fredrich. *Herr Eugen Dühring's Revolution in Science.* New York: International Publishers, no date.

Fox-Genovese, Elizabeth. *The Origins of Physiocracy.* Ithaca: Cornell University Press, 1976.

Gide, Charles and Rist, Charles. *A History of Economic Doctrines.* Boston: D.C. Heath and Company, 1949.

Gleicher, David. "The Historical Bases of Physiocracy: An Analysis of the *Tableau Économique,*" *Science and Society,* 46 (Fall 1982), 328-360.

185

Gray, Sir Alexander and Thompson, Alan. *The Development of Economic Doctrine.* 2nd ed. New York: Longman, 1980.

Harrod, Roy F. "An Essay in Dynamic Theory," *Economic Journal,* 49 (March 1939), 14-33.

Harrod, Roy F. *Towards a Dynamic Economics.* London: MacMillan, 1948.

Heckscher, Eli F. *Mercantilism.* 2 vols. London: George Allen and Unwin Ltd., 1933.

Higgs, Henry. *The Physiocrats.* London: MacMillan & Co., 1897.

Hunt, E.K. *History of Economic Thought: A Critical Perspective.* Belmont: Wadsworth, 1979.

Jones, Hywel G. *An Introduction to Modern Theories of Economic Growth.* New York: McGraw-Hill, 1976.

Kaldor, Nicholas. *Strategic Factors in Economic Development.* Ithaca: Cornell University Press, 1967.

Keynes, John Maynard. *The General Theory of Employment, Interest and Money.* New York: Harcourt, Brace and World, 1964.

Kuczynski, Marguerita and Meek, Ronald L., eds. *Quesnay's Tableau Économique.* New York: Augustus M. Kelley, 1972.

Landreth, Harry. *History of Economic Theory.* Boston: Houghton Mifflin, 1976.

Leibenstein, Harvey. *Beyond Economic Man: A New Foundation for Microeconomics.* Cambridge: Cambridge University Press, 1976.

Leonteif, Wassily. *Input-Output Economics.* New York: Oxford University Press, 1966.

Leonteif, Wassily. *The Structure of the American Economy, 1919-1929.* Cambridge: Harvard University Press, 1941.

Malthus, Thomas Robert. *Population: The First Essay.* Ann Arbor: University of Michigan Press, 1959.

Malthus, Thomas Robert. *Principles of Political Economy.* New York: Augustus M. Kelley, 1951.

Marshall, Alfred. *Principles of Economics.* 8th ed. New York: Macmillan and Co., 1947.

Marx, Karl. *Capital.* 3 vols. New York: International Publishers, 1967.

Marx, Karl. *Theories of Surplus Value.* 3 vols. Moscow: Foreign Language Publishing House, 1954.

Meek, Ronald L. *The Economics of Physiocracy.* Cambridge: Harvard University Press, 1963.

Meek, Ronald L. "Problems of the *Tableau Économique*," *Economica*, 27 (November 1960), 322-347.

Mill, James. *Elements of Political Economy*. 3rd ed. London: Henry G. Bohn, 1844.

Mill, John Stuart. *Principles of Political Economy*. 2 vols. New York: D. Appleton and Company, 1895.

Mirabeau, Victor de Riquetti, Marquis de and Quesnay, François. *L'Ami des Hommes*. 5 vols. Avignon, 1762.

Pasinetti, Luigi L. *Lectures on the Theory of Production*. New York: Columbia University Press, 1977.

Phillips, Almarin. "The Tableau Économique as a Simple Leontief Model," *Quarterly Journal of Economics*, 69 (February 1955), 137-44.

Pressman, Steven. "Quesnay's Theory of Economic Growth and Decline," in *Economics as Worldly Philosophy*, ed. Ron Blackwell, Jaspal Chatha and Edward J. Nell (London: Macmillan, 1993), 305-321

Pressman, Steven. "Review of The Economics of François Quesnay by Gianni Vaggi," *History of Political Economy*, 23 (Fall 1991), 551-552.

Quesnay, François. *The Economical Table*. New York: Bergman Publishers, 1968.

Quesnay, François. *François Quesnay et la Physiocratie*. Paris: Institut National d'Etudes Demographiques, 1958.

Quesnay, Francois. *Philosophie Rurale*. 5 vols. Amsterdam: Chez Les Libraires Associes, 1764.

Ricardo, David. *The Principles of Political Economy and Taxation*. New York: Dutton, 1973.

Routh, Guy. *The Origin of Economic Ideas*. New York: Random House, 1975.

Samuels, Warren J. "The Physiocratic Theory of Economic Policy," *Quarterly Journal of Economics*, 76 (February 1962), 145-162.

Samuelson, Paul A. "Quesnay's 'Tableau Économique' as a Theorist would Formulate it Today," in *Classical and Marxian Political Economy*, ed. Ian Bradley and Michael Howard. New York: St. Martin's Press, 1982.

Schumpeter, Joseph A. *Economic Doctrine and Method*. New York: Oxford University Press, 1954.

Schumpeter, Joseph A. *History of Economic Analysis*. New York: Oxford University Press, 1954.

Shackle, G.L.S. *The Years of High Theory*. Cambridge: Cambridge

188   QUESNAY'S TABLEAU ÉCONOMIQUE

University Press, 1978.
Smith, Adam. *The Wealth of Nations.* New York: Modern Library, 1937.
Spengler, Joseph J. "Mercantilist and Physiocratic Growth Theory," in Bert Hoselitz et. al. *Theories of Economic Growth.* Glencoe: Free Press, 1960.
Sraffa, Piero. *Production of Commodites by Means of Commodities.* Cambridge: Cambridge University Press, 1960.
Steuart, Sir James. *An Inquiry into the Principles of Political Economy,* Vols. I-IV of *The Works of Sir James Steuart.* New York: Augustus M. Kelley, 1967.
Sweezy, Paul. *The Theory of Capitalist Development.* New York: Monthly Review Press, 1942.
Vaggi, Gianni. *The Economics of François Quesnay.* Durham, N.C.: Duke University Press, 1987.
Vaggi, Gianni. "A Physiocratic Model of Relative Prices and Income Distribution," *Economic Journal,* 95 (December 1985), 928-947.
Vaggi, Gianni. "The Role of Profits in Physiocratic Economics," *History of Political Economy,* 17 (Fall 1985), 367-384.
Vaggi, Gianni. "Surplus and Effective Demand in Physiocracy," *Studi economi,* n. 18 (1982), 55-90.
Walsh, Vivan and Gram, Harvey. *Classical and Neoclassical Theories of General Equilibrium.* New York: Oxford University Press, 1980.
Woog, Henri. *The Tableau Économique of François Quesnay.* Bern: A Francke A.G. Verlag, 1950.

INDEX